Las Vegas

A Pictorial Celebration
Michael S. Green, Ph.D.

Photography by Elan Penn

Sterling Publishing Co., Inc.
New York

Design by Michel Opatowski
Edited by J. E. Sigler
Layout by Gala Pre Press Ltd.

Penn Publishing gratefully acknowledges the following institutions and individuals for allowing photographs from their collections to be reproduced in this book: Bally's Las Vegas 64-65. Bellagio Las Vegas 97. Caesars Palace 61. Chris Farina/Corbis 136. Cummins Richard/Corbis 1, 3, 62, 68-69, 70-71. U.S. Department of Energy 54-56. Flamingo Las Vegas 66-67. Leynse James/Corbis 1, 76. MGM Grand Hotel & Casino Las Vegas 85. Mirage Hotel & Casino Las Vegas 80-81. New York-New York Hotel & Casino Las Vegas 87. Paris Las Vegas Hotel 95. Treasure Island Hotel & Casino 83. University of Nevada Las Vegas: Alicia Lawrence Collection 12, Dennis McBride Collection 21, Ferron Collection 16, Helen J. Stewart Collection 8, Las Vegas News Bureau Collection 11, 13, 15, Manis Collection 18, 20, 23, Maurine & Fred Wilson Collection 10, North Las Vegas Library Collection 17, Rockwell Collection 6-7, Sands Hotel Collection 9, 14, 19.

Library of Congress Cataloging-in-Publication Data

Green, Michael S.
Las Vegas: a pictorial celebration / Michael S. Green ; photography by Elan Penn.
p. cm.
ISBN 1-4027-2385-7
1. Las Vegas (Nev.)-Description and travel.2. Las Vegas (Nev.)-Pictorial works. 3. Las (Nev.)-Building, structures, etc. I. Penn, Elan. II. Title.

F849.L35G74 2005
917.93'135-dc22

2005049945

2 4 6 8 10 9 7 5 3 1

Published by Sterling Publishing Co., Inc.
387 Park Avenue South, New York, NY 10016
© 2005 by © Penn Publishing Ltd.
Distributed in Canada by Sterling Publishing
c/o Canadian Manda Group, 165 Dufferin Street
Toronto, Ontario, Canada M6K 3H6
Distributed in Great Britain by Chrysalis Books Group PLC
The Chrysalis Building, Bramley Road, London W10 6SP, England
Distributed in Australia by Capricorn Link (Australia) Pty. Ltd.
P.O. Box 704, Windsor, NSW 2756, Australia

Sterling ISBN 1-4027-2385-7

For information about custom editions, special sales, premium and corporate purchases, please contact Sterling Special Sales Department at 800-805-5489 or specialsales@sterlingpub.com.

Opposite: Signs advertising games at the Riviera Hotel & Casino

Contents

Las Vegas: City of Living Legends

Las Vegas Springs, early 1900s: The Big Springs or Las Vegas Springs provided an oasis in the desert for travelers on the Old Spanish Trail—and a water supply for early residents.

Sin City. City of Lights. Entertainment Capital of the World. Las Vegas is called by all these names, and they are accurate—as far as they go. About 37 million visitors from around the world flock to Las Vegas each year to sample its pleasures: not just gambling, but also dining, entertainment, shopping, and a pleasant desert climate. Those who visit once might return to a place they hardly recognize, though. The city is an American cultural landmark and international icon, but it has never had any qualms with (literally) blowing up parts of its past to boldly try new themes and approaches. It has become known as a place that constantly reinvents itself, and that's more than just a part of the Las Vegas charm: it's the

very secret that keeps the city perpetually exciting.

Yet these fleeting elements are only details of the greater Las Vegas story. The city and its surroundings are unique in that they have been shaped not just by locals and events that occurred a few blocks from the Strip, but also by distant events and people from thousands of miles away. Money, madness, the mob, near-mythical characters—these are the things the legendary city is made of. But Las Vegas also has a very real side, a side made up of everyday, average Americans with community centers, churches, and schools. The sometimes delicate, sometimes wild dance of this living city with the legendary one is the true story of Las Vegas, and that's what this book promises to tell.

Old Las Vegas: From Desert Spring to Railroad Station

Though 2005 marks its centennial, Las Vegas is actually eons old, geologically speaking. The red sandstone that earned Valley of Fire and Red Rock Canyon their names testify to the earthquakes and erosion that shaped this part of the Mojave Desert. Petroglyphs and other markings left by Basket Maker peoples and other hunter-gatherers provide evidence that people lived in southern Nevada as early as 3,000 years ago. Around 700 AD, the peaceful

Las Vegas Spring on the desert which makes a stream of over 300 cubic inches of water.

Ranch house, Las Vegas Fort (Stewart Ranch), early 1900s. The Mormon Fort became known as the Las Vegas Ranch after the missionaries left. This is as it looked around the time owner Helen J. Stewart sold the ranch and the land around it to railroad builder William A. Clark.

Opposite: If they look like they were having fun, they were: from left, Dean Martin, Sammy Davis Jr., Peter Lawford, Frank Sinatra, and Joey Bishop at the Summit at the Sands.

tribe that is still most closely associated with this area of the Southwest, the Paiutes, apparently moved into southern Nevada. Just as it would be for all future settlers here, this portion of the desert's natural springs and flowing waters are what attracted the natives to the site.

The first known non-Native American visitor to the Las Vegas Valley, Rafael Rivera, was a scout who worked for New Mexico trader Antonio Armijo. On January 7, 1830, Armijo's company camped a few miles southeast of today's Strip. Their travels established Las Vegas—Spanish for "the meadows"—as a stop on the Old Spanish Trail from New Mexico to southern California, but Las Vegas still remained little known until John Frémont's arrival. A captain in the US

Army's mapmaking corps, Frémont came through the valley on May 2 and 3, 1844. It was his best-selling report of his travels through what were then Mexico's northern provinces that brought Las Vegas its first dose of real attention.

It was also Frémont's report that Brigham Young used to guide the Mormons west to Salt Lake City in the 1840s. In 1855, Young chose Las Vegas for a mission and dispatched a 30-man party there. They built what is now known as Mormon Fort, but stayed less than three years. The fort survived as a supply depot for nearby miners, then as the Las Vegas Ranch, until it was sold in 1902 to Senator William Clark, a Montana copper baron who wanted to build the San Pedro, Los Angeles & Salt Lake Railroad there. Passenger service began with the railroad's completion on May 1, 1905, and just two weeks later, about 3,000 gathered in 110-degree heat for an auction of lots in what is now downtown Las Vegas. That day is considered the city's birth date.

Old Las Vegas: From Railroad Station to Federal Town

In 1909, the legislature created Clark County (named for the senator who built the railroad),

Above: Property auction, Las Vegas, 15th May, 1905. This auction is considered the beginning of Las Vegas. The temperature that day reached 110 degrees—hot enough even without the suits and dresses worn by the crowd.

Opposite: When Liberace made an entrance, he really made an entrance. Small wonder that he was known as "Mr. Showmanship.".

with Las Vegas as county seat, giving the new town small-scale clerical and licensing services. Various settlers came together to create businesses ranging from banks to telephone companies, beginning a local trend that continues to this day: money and power in a few hands. Buy-outs were common even in those days, and in 1921 the Union Pacific bought out Clark's railroad. Shortly thereafter, railroad workers organized a nationwide strike that Las Vegans strongly supported. After the strike ended, the Union Pacific moved its Las Vegas repair shops north to Caliente, denying any intent to punish the heavily unionized town. Las Vegans had to find a new way to prosper.

Luckily for them, the federal government had its eye on the desert star. After two decades of study and negotiation, the seven states sharing the Colorado River agreed to divide its waters. Congress soon approved the idea, and in March

1931 construction began on what was originally known as the Boulder Canyon Project—now known as Hoover Dam.

The project's impact on Las Vegas was enormous. With the Great Depression on, thousands migrated to southern Nevada in search of a job, and the majority stayed. Dam workers lived in Boulder City, a federal reservation created by the government to house them—and to control them. Reservation policy banned all forms of vice, and so, every payday, dam workers dying to let loose filled the highway to Las Vegas. They weren't alone, either: Even while the dam was still in construction, hundreds of thousands of tourists flocked to see what was being called "the eighth wonder of the world." Once they saw it, they too headed for Las Vegas.

The federal government continued to bring benefits to Las Vegas. A new federal building was built in the 1930s, signifying growth and permanence. Franklin Roosevelt's New Deal modernized the community with a new city park, sewer lines, pavement, and other amenities. Friends in high federal places also helped the town that had helped them: Pat McCarran owed his 1932 US Senate election partly to Las Vegas support, and he delivered several federal projects to Las Vegas during World War II. Those projects

Opposite: Ann-Margret was the darling of Las Vegas entertainment when she posed for this publicity shot for the Las Vegas News Bureau.

Below: Fremont Street with banner across street, Union Pacific Depot at end of street, circa 1930s. Las Vegas advertised its connection to the eighth wonder of the world while Hoover Dam was under construction.

created jobs, jobs drew new residents, and new residents meant growth.

Another federal installation brought Las Vegas more attention, jobs, and residents—but this one had unintended consequences as well. Late in 1950, the Atomic Energy Commission chose land northwest of Las Vegas as a test site for atomic bombs. Las Vegas officials and entrepreneurs turned the phenomenon into a tourist attraction, but those who lived downwind during the 120 aboveground tests conducted until 1963 suffered from a series of health problems they blamed on exposure to radiation. The govermment denies to this day that the radiation injured their health, a fact that frustrates many locals. Certain of that danger as only eyewitnesses can be, Las Vegans have preferred to end the friendly, welcoming relationship with their federal government rather than continue on as its chosen city in the Southwest.

The Old Strip: From Siegel to Caesars

As the payday adventures of the Hoover Dam workers testify, Las Vegas always had something more than just federal jobs to offer. Back when the railroad first checked out of town, Las Vegans wised up to their dependence on non-local companies and started contriving ways to "diversify their economy," as they say today. For the first time, they realized that the town's racy reputation—instead of bringing shame to the locals—might just be able to bring them a livelihood. All the way back to the days of horse thieves on the trail, the West had been known for its wild adventures—but Las Vegas was known for being especially good at them.

Originally, the railroad banned liquor sales anywhere except Block 16 (along First Street between Stewart and Ogden) and in hotels. In response, many businesses off the block simply added a room, claimed to be a hotel, and continued selling alcohol. Faced with this competition, the early saloons of Block 16 upped the ante: they too added rooms, but for prostitutes. That's how the oldest profession arrived in Las Vegas, but, more importantly, the "one-upmanship" that ushered it in established very early on the pattern that is now recognized as "typical Las Vegas": local businessmen are always trying to build something newer, bigger, better, more amazing (or shocking) than anything the competition has. And that draws tourists.

Opposite: Copa Girl Linda Lawson as "Mis-Cue" Wearing A-bomb crown, 1950s. Surrounded by six servicemen, Sands Copa Girl Linda Lawson served as "Mis-Cue" in honor of the misfired Operation Cue Bomb, evidence of ties between Las Vegas tourism and nearby atomic testing.

Here's a trio to draw to! Tom Jones, Priscilla Presley . . . and the King.

Under that impression, and under economic pressure from the loss of the railroad repair shops, Las Vegans began expanding their attractions in the 1920s. Western Air Express soon began providing daily passenger air service to and from Las Vegas. Then, in 1931—as part of a conscious effort to attract visitors who might decide they liked the state enough to stay, invest, and become taxpayers—state legislators passed two laws that revolutionized Nevada. One cut the residency requirement for divorce to six weeks, the lowest in the US. The other eliminated most restrictions on gambling.

That worked. Between the passage of the law

and 1958, most of the old Strip and downtown was forged. Encouraged by the success of the very first such resorts, the now-legendary El Rancho Vegas and Last Frontier, investors from other states moved in and built the Flamingo, Thunderbird, Desert Inn, Sands, Sahara, Riviera, Dunes, New Frontier, Royal Nevada, Hacienda, Tropicana, and Stardust. The owners of these establishments imported talented big-name entertainers whom most of them knew from their days in other jurisdictions. Most notable was the Sands, which became famed for the 1960 "Rat Pack" summit featuring Frank Sinatra, Dean Martin, and Sammy Davis, Jr. The new

Meadows Country Club, color postcard, circa 1930s. The Meadows was the first local "carpet joint," built by bootleggers from Southern California.

resorts were able to offer cheap (or reasonably priced) entertainment, food, rooms, and shopping, all because the plan called for the real profits to be made in the casino—and they were.

Usually, Strip entrepreneurs shared a common background: most of them were Jewish, and most had gotten into (or were in) scrapes with the law running illegal casinos elsewhere. They welcomed the chance for legitimacy in Las Vegas, where their trade was legal, and as if they were eager to show their graciousness for that chance, they contributed very generously to community causes—not just the local temple, in which several of them were involved, but everything from a cathedral next to the Desert Inn to

the local United Way. They were not all rehabilitated criminals, however: Some still pursued illegal activities, from illegal gambling elsewhere to drug trafficking and money laundering.

As most people know, legislation is not entirely responsible for the Strip's growth. It also had a lot to do with vision, luck, and muscle. In the late 1960s, two men in particular proved that truth: Jay Sarno and Howard Hughes. Sarno, a motel chain operator, opened Caesars, with its ancient Roman theme, and the Circus Circus, with its big-top circus theme. Strip hotels hadn't offered a theme since the 1940s, but, thanks to Sarno, that tradition would return with a vengeance.

To Hughes is credited—at least by many—the removal of organized crime from the city. In truth, he did buy out corrupt owners among his many Las Vegas acquisitions, but he also kept employees who had been skimming money—and kept doing it. The perception and the reality about Hughes differ, but it is undeniable that he brought Las Vegas newfound respectability, however much or little deserved it was. "If it was good enough for Hughes," they used to say, "it was good enough for Wall Street."

Indeed, thanks to a third change in the 1960s, Wall Street could now invest. Under previous Nevada law, every stockholder in a casino had to be licensed, a stipulation that blocked a publicly traded corporation with thousands of stockholders from owning any Las Vegas property. The new Corporate Gaming Act of 1969, which required licenses only for key stockholders and executives, finally enabled corporations to own casinos. In turn, corporations from outside Nevada entered the market—Hilton and Kirk Kerkorian's MGM, for example—and the Reno-based company Harrah's became the first Nevada gaming firm to incorporate and go on the stock market.

Though corporate gaming reduced mob influ-

Walter Cronkite was "the most trusted man in America," and Siegfried & Roy felt that he could be trusted with one of their lion cubs.

Fremont Street, circa 1940s. Fremont Street remained the center of town in the 1940s, with most of the town's most prominent casinos—and servicemen signifying the country at war and international events that would transform Las Vegas.

ence, critics feared that organized crime would use corporations as fronts. Argent proved them right: The corporation owned the Stardust, Fremont, and Hacienda, and turned out to be a front for Chicago, Milwaukee, and Kansas City organized-crime bosses represented by Frank Rosenthal, as depicted in the film *Casino*. Corporate owners of the Tropicana and Aladdin were also organized-crime fronts. Only after state officials had forced out Argent—and its mob-connected successor—did Boyd Gaming take over the Stardust and Fremont, finally driving organized-crime ownership out of Las Vegas.

The New Strip: Megaresorts, Mergers, and Money

Now Las Vegas was poised for its next boom. By this time, however, the national scene had changed: New Jersey had legalized gambling in Atlantic City in the late 1970s, and others had followed with riverboat and land-based casinos, as well as lotteries and casinos owned by Indian tribes but often run by gaming corporations. Las Vegas would have to change, too, if it was going to deal with the new competition.

In 1973, the main architect of that change, Steve Wynn, took over and dramatically enhanced the downtown Golden Nugget. That was just an introduction, though. It was Wynn's Mirage, opened in November 1989, that revolutionized the industry. Not only was the building far larger than its counterparts, but Wynn's arrangement with illusionists Siegfried and Roy, longtime Las Vegas performers, extended far beyond the usual scope of Strip entertainment and the average cost of a show.

The next year, the Excalibur opened not far away with a very different approach. The new hotel-casino featured a medieval England–King

Opposite: Color postcard—Hotel Last Frontier, circa 1940s. The Hotel Last Frontier opened in 1942 as the Strip's second resort and continued the western theme that then dominated Las Vegas.

El Rancho Vegas, circa 1940s.
It was not necessarily normal in the 1940s that the El Rancho Vegas was fully air-conditioned. It was the first hotel-casino on what became the Las Vegas Strip.

Arthur theme, just like the Mirage's rain forest, but it targeted customers with less cash and younger family members. Coupled with Wynn's more up-scale image, the two properties represented the two different marketing models upon which the rest of the coming boom would base itself.

And, oh! What a boom! First, Wynn built the Treasure Island and the Bellagio. Then Circus Circus erected the Excalibur, the Luxor, and Mandalay Bay. The success of these establishments inspired others: Sheldon

3B-H751

Adelson and his stunning, all-suite Venetian; Park Place's Paris Las Vegas, complete with a replica of the Eiffel Tower; and Kerkorian's new MGM Grand, the largest hotel in the world at its opening, and then his New York–New York.

But the latest hallmark of the New Strip is not themes or corporate ownership. It's that greatest of capitalistic achievements: buying out the competition. Indeed, the list of Strip buy-outs and mergers is long and dizzying: Park Place joined Bally's, then took over Hilton's casino operations, then merged with Caesars Entertainment, which now proposes to merge with Harrah's. In 2004, Kerkorian's MGM Mirage owned the Mirage, Treasure Island, Bellagio, MGM Grand, New York–New York, and half of the Monte Carlo—and then came a nearly $9 billion merger with Mandalay Resort Group that gave Kerkorian ownership of nine of the Strip's largest resorts. Big players, big stakes, big wins—that's just a regular day on the New Strip.

Other Sides of the Strip: Fun Without Gambling!

Believe it or not, the Strip always has been more than the megaresorts that line the street. Resort restaurants, shops, clubs, sports amenities—even entire theme parks—have catered to both travelers and locals since the very beginning. But just as the hotels of the last few years have become larger and more elaborate than their predecessors, so have their neighboring Strip "extras." Shopping, for instance, became a true Strip event with the creation of the Forum Shoppes by Caesars Palace in 1992. Since then, other malls have opened nearby, offering everything from elaborate, up-scale style, like at the recently renovated Fashion Show mall, to a more modest, recently renovated atmosphere, like at the Showcase Mall.

The other sides of the Strip have also become one of the best reflections of the new approach adopted by casino-owners in the early 1990s: that of family-friendliness. Many of the millions

Wilbur Clark's Desert Inn, 1950s. The vintage cars and vintage hotel are a reminder of Las Vegas as it was. The Desert Inn was the class of the Strip when it opened in 1950.

who visit Las Vegas each year find themselves walking or driving around the Strip's four miles—and, sometimes to their surprise, they find fun things to do besides gambling. Many hotel-casinos added theme parks, rides, roller coasters, and zoo-like features during the '90s. Both Bellagio and Wynn Las Vegas feature art galleries, and the Venetian even has a Guggenheim art gallery. Gameworks is nothing but fun and games, and the Elvis-A-Rama and Liberace Museums nearby provide visitors with two chances to worship at the shrines of the most popular Las Vegas entertainers ever. Thanks to Las Vegas' never-ending effort to live up to its nickname, "The Entertainment Capital of the World," no guest of this city—no matter how old—should ever need utter those frightful words: "I'm bored."

Downtown and Beyond: More Gambling, Different Neighborhood

Most people don't know that the Strip is not Las Vegas' downtown. In fact, the Strip is not technically even within the city limits! And while the Strip has undergone a couple of booms, the real downtown's main thoroughfare, Fremont Street, has also continued to evolve. Its first casinos in the 1930s were tiny compared with the Strip's megaresorts, but the two shared characteristics both with one another and with today's business. Just as modern owners like Dalitz, Hughes, and Kerkorian extended their reach beyond the casino business, operators of early downtown casinos were businessmen often involved in other enterprises. Also, even if they were less elaborate than the Strip's pyramids and volcanoes, downtown casinos in the 1930s featured Old Western themes, from cowboys and Indians to pioneers and gold-rushers.

In the late 1930s, downtown even experienced its own little boom when state officials began driving operators of illegal casinos out of California. Many of those evicted from the Golden State came to Las Vegas, including the builders of the Golden Nugget, El Cortez, and several other Western-oriented casinos. The expansion of downtown by Californians began drawing investors from other states as well. In 1951, veteran Texas gambler Benny Binion opened his pride and joy, the Horseshoe, and five years later one of his partners, Sands co-owner Ed Levinson, opened the Fremont.

In time, downtown Las Vegas faced the same fate as many other cities' urban cores: the loss of businesses and residents to newer parts of town and suburbs. But the neighborhood did manage to remain the center of local government, and hotel construction continued. What made downtown gaming a harder sell was the spread of local casinos throughout the valley in the 1980s. This phenomenon started with the birth of Frank Fertitta's locals' casino empire, the Station Casinos, and has spread like wildfire as other downtown operators have branched out into neighborhood gambling.

As Las Vegas gaming became more corporate, hope was born downtown that the area, though it had long lagged behind the Strip, could now carve out a niche of its own. Indeed, downtown has changed: In 1995, local government and casino owners built the Fremont Street Experience, a canopy that turned the street into a pedestrian mall and actually drew tourists away from the Strip to watch its hourly light show. In the '90s and early 2000s, talk of serious downtown redevelopment began. Some results are already beginning to appear, but the dreams for downtown are big and will likely take a while to come to fruition. As fast as things change around here, though . . . who really can know?

The Real Las Vegas: (Mostly) Normal Places to Live and Go

The efforts to develop downtown are reminders that Las Vegas is, after all, a place to live. The city itself is small, with a population of about only 600,000, but with a great deal of land that includes downtown and many acres west of the old railroad tracks. Like many cities, Las Vegas has seen quite a lot of suburban growth and migration. During the late twentieth century, ambitious developers challenged themselves to turn the industrial areas and vast empty tracts of land just outside the city into elite, master-planned suburban communities. Summerlin, Henderson, Green Valley, the Lakes, Lake Las Vegas, and North Las Vegas are now some of the nation's most popular places to live. Though many of their residents are not technically within the city limits, they often consider themselves Las Vegans as much as any downtown-dweller. With all these self-proclaimed Las Vegans included, the urban area actually totals about 1.7 million, and population experts project that number will double by 2020.

Each month, Las Vegas gains an average 7,000 new residents, and loses about 3,000. Those coming and going do not always vacate and fill in the same neighborhoods, and Clark County faces a considerable challenge just trying to create a sense of community among such a rapidly changing population. The county currently boasts the nation's fifth-largest school district, but it opens an average of one new school per month. In the late 1980s and early 1990s, the Las Vegas–Clark County Library District considerably expanded its programs and services and even built several new branches, one of which became the new permanent home of the Las Vegas Art Museum. Not long ago, the city got a second public radio station, and the University of Nevada, Las Vegas and the Community College of Southern Nevada host community and cultural events practically every day. Las Vegas boasts plenty of sports entertainment, too: From the valley's many parks and various leagues to local auto races and annual major league baseball exhibition games at Cashman Field Center, Clark County manages to keep its athletes fit and its sports fans entertained—even in the middle of the desert.

Beyond the Lights: Day-Trips from Las Vegas

Most visitors to Las Vegas leave without seeing much more than the Strip's casinos and resort hotels. Many don't even know that there's anything else to be seen in Las Vegas itself, much less that there's a state full of communities and scenic vistas beyond the lights. Some such communities are tourist resorts in their own right: Mesquite, Laughlin, and Primm, for example, offer casino gambling as well as hotels that boast everything from spas to big-name entertainment. Other sites, however, offer a welcome break from gambling and shopping. Located in the middle of the Mojave Desert, Las Vegas is just a short drive from the stark beauty of Death Valley and the awe-inspiring magnificence of the Grand Canyon. Both are favorite getaway spots for locals, but they also attract a significant number of Las Vegas visitors who want to see the nearby natural wonders known throughout the world.

A trip out to these places is not only rewarding in itself, it makes clear to the visitor just how isolated Las Vegas really is—and thus how great the achievement of the original city builders really was. True, there were some criminals among those builders, and because of them Las Vegas has long been considered a haven for political and financial corruption. The city was corrupt, in fact—but that corruption stemmed mostly from small-town cronyism, not East-coast mobs. Recent growth has led to more indictments, bribery charges, and ethics complaints, but those problems are already no longer Las Vegas' primary ones. Out-of-control population growth and its terrible strain on the desert water supply are. Alas, those are not juicy media stories, and so the legend of the great mob oasis in the Mojave lives on.

As for the real Las Vegas, it's used to catching flak for problems that all towns have. Its good and bad moments are played out on a stage much larger than cities of similar size, but, as the city's first entrepreneurs recognized, the same reputation that draws unwanted attention also draws the crowds—and so nobody really complains. In 1900, with just 30 residents, this town was nothing more than a place for weary travelers to stop. With more than 1.7 million residents today, Las Vegas has become the place the whole world wants to go.

Old Las Vegas: From Desert Spring to Railroad Station

Valley of Fire

Once upon a time, southern Nevada was an area of great seismic activity, with faults, earthquakes, and erosion. About 150 million years ago, shifting sand dunes formed the area now known as the Valley of Fire. Humans started visiting the area about 2,300 years ago, but they tended to live in the nearby Moapa Valley, where water was far more abundant. The Anasazi—whose way of life can be explored at the nearby Lost City Museum—farmed in the Moapa Valley for hundreds of years, but appear to have used the Valley of Fire only for hunting, gathering, rock art, and religious ceremonies.

One of the valley's more famous—and more modern—residents was a renegade half-Mexican, half-Indian known as Mouse. During the 1890s, while on a drunken spree, Mouse killed at least two men and shot several others, then fled to the Valley of Fire to hide from the authorities. The part of Petroglyph Canyon in which he hid off and on for about six months is now known as "Mouse's Tank."

The valley boasts the honor of being the founding member of the Nevada State Park System, created in 1935. It was named for its red sandstone, although visitors will also see plenty of limestone and shales right beside the sandstone. The great rocks are home to many cacti and other desert plants, as well as various birds, lizards, snakes, and small game. Tourists even see

Previous page: Northeast corner of Mormont Fort,
State Historic Park.

One of many fine examples of prehistoric Indian rock writing on Petroglyph Canyon Trail.

an occasional desert tortoise, an endangered species. For locals, the site is a pleasant drive northeast of town and a fine place for a picnic— except during the summer, when temperatures there often top 120 degrees. For Hollywood, the Valley of Fire is an ideal spot for location shooting: In 1939, Hal Roach Studios filmed *One Million, B.C.*, and *Star Trek* fans will immediately recognize the Silica Dome area from *Star Trek: Generations*.

Red Rock Canyon

Located west of town, the approximately 130-square-mile Red Rock Canyon National Conservation Area is a favorite hiking spot for Las Vegans, and enough tourists have found it to send its visitor count above 1.2 million a year. Its 13-mile loop is especially appealing to bicyclists, but many simply drive through to briefly take in its scenic wonders—especially Calico Vista, which has a spectacular view of the Aztec sandstone located below the look-out. With mountains as high as 8,000 feet, the canyon is truly prime hiking ground, but it offers less

rigorous pleasures as well, including a variety of desert plants, endangered desert tortoises, and burros, a small wild donkey that is protected under the Wild Horse and Burro Act of 1971.

Geologically, Red Rock's history is similar to that of the Valley of Fire. Native Americans also inhabited the Red Rock Canyon area, partly because there were springs here—even centuries ago, water determined a great deal of Las Vegas' history. As they did in the Valley of Fire, the Anasazi and Paiutes left behind rock art and artifacts in the canyon. Especially in the Willow Spring picnic area and near the start of the Keystone Thrust Trail (a reference to a thrust

fault that helped shape the area), many shards of pottery and roasting pits have been found. Roasting pits were used for cooking plants and animals, and at least one has been found in the canyon that is as large as 27 feet across!

Not far from Red Rock Canyon are Bonnie Springs Old Nevada, an Old West-style theme park, and the Spring Mountain Ranch State Park, a site with a long and fascinating history whose owners have included Vera Krupp (owner of the world-famous Krupp Diamond) and Howard Hughes. A day trip out from the city should provide enough time to see all three, and those who make the journey never regret that they did so.

The Springs Preserve

Native Americans dwelled at the Las Vegas Springs for thousands of years before, in 1844, John Frémont stopped there during his western mapmaking expedition. His best-selling travel report noted the warm springs that bubbled to the surface from underground aquifers and the lush grass surrounding them—which helped explain to his readers why the Spanish and Mexicans had long referred to the area as *Las Vegas*, "the meadows."

At that time, a creek flowed from the springs across the northern and eastern portion of the valley, running right by the fort-mission that Mormons built there in 1855. The stream remained visible long after the town's founding in 1905, but dried up in the 1930s. The Las Vegas Springs—or Big Springs, as they were also known—provided the bulk of Las Vegas' water supply for more than half a century, but city residents were wasteful and depleted the aquifer, forcing local officials to draw increasingly from the Colorado River and Hoover Dam.

The springs are on what is now Las Vegas Valley Water District land in the western portion of Las Vegas, near Interstate 95 and Valley View. In 2006, the Springs Preserve will open there. Mayor Oscar Goodman has hoped that the new project will become for Las Vegas what Central Park is for New York, albeit a bit less green and lush, for obvious reasons. It will include a great diversity of facilities, including trails and desert gardens; two large amphitheaters for programs and performances, one seating 500 and the other 2,000; and a 70,000-square-foot desert living center showing people how they can make wiser use of water and energy. Eventually, the Nevada State Museum and Historical Society, now located in Lorenzi Park, will also move there. Ideally, this relocation will restore to the Las Vegas Springs its age-old—but long-overlooked—reputation as the center of southern Nevada history.

Mormon Fort

Las Vegas was already a well-known pit stop for travelers when Mormon church leader Brigham Young decided to send missionaries here from Great Salt Lake. On June 14, 1855, 30 Mormon men arrived under the leadership of William Bringhurst. They built their fort-mission next to the creek that used to flow from the Las Vegas Springs and set up an experimental farm about a mile away to teach the local Paiutes new farming techniques. The mission produced enough food for the men to send back to Salt Lake for their families, but a variety of problems would end the settlement in less than three years. First, after a few of the men found a nearby lead outcropping, they bickered over whether they should be mining or farming. Secondly, the cottonwood trees surrounding the mission and the nearby creek couldn't provide nearly enough shelter from the oppressive summer heat. Then, in 1857, Young called home all Mormons outside the Utah territory to defend their Zion from US soldiers sent to enforce their obedience to federal law.

For several years after the Mormons' departure, the Las Vegas mission served as a supply depot for miners. For the rest of the nineteenth century, however, the fort would be owned by two families as the Las Vegas Ranch. California Gold Rush miner Octavius Decatur Gass was the first to recognize the old fort's possibilities, and from 1865 to 1881 he ran a successful ranch there, growing crops and raising cattle with help from Paiute ranchhands. During that time, Gass

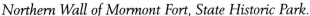

Northern Wall of Mormont Fort, State Historic Park.

Adobe house, only surviving structure from the original 1855 fort.

persuaded an old friend from his native Ohio, Conrad Kiel, to join him in the Las Vegas area.

When legal and financial troubles finally forced Gass to sell the ranch to Archibald Stewart, Kiel suspected that Stewart had swindled Gass out of his ranch. What was worse, Kiel's ranch, about a mile away, was a haven for outlaws and gunslingers. In June 1884, after a Stewart ranchhand insulted Helen Stewart and went to work for Kiel, Archibald rode over to the Kiel Ranch. Soon, Helen Stewart received a note from Kiel that her husband was dead. An inquest found that his killer had acted in self-defense, but Helen never believed it nor spoke again to Kiel or his two sons, who inherited his ranch. Helen—a 30-year-old widow with four children and one on the way—remained to run her ranch. She hired foremen to help her and eventually married one of them. One day in 1900, her second husband rode with one of her sons over to the Kiel Ranch, where they found both of Kiel's sons shot to death. The original finding of a murder-suicide has been disproved, but the killer remains

unknown. One plausible theory points to a Stewart son.

In 1902, Mrs. Stewart sold about 1,800 acres of her land, including the ranch, to Montana copper baron William Andrews Clark, who would soon build a railroad through the area. For most of Las Vegas' early years after the 1905 land auction that created the town, the ranch served as a resort, with a swimming hole to escape the summer heat. When construction on Hoover Dam was about to begin, the Bureau of Reclamation began using the site for chemical experiments related to that project. In the 1930s, the old fort-mission fell into disrepair and remained mostly abandoned until the city gave control of the site—the oldest building in Nevada—to the state in 1991, which turned it into a state park. Only one of the original walls built by the Mormon settlers still stands, but Clark County voters approved several bond issues and the state legislature provided funding to build replicas of the fort walls and corral, and in 2005 a new visitor center provided space for more exhibits on the fort-mission's fascinating history.

Downtown Paiute Colony

The Paiutes are a Native American tribe that has lived in southern Nevada for nearly two millennia. Archaeologists estimate they arrived in the region possibly as early as 300 AD, but they definitely were here by 700 AD. For several centuries they shared the land with the Anasazi, who tended to reside closer to the rivers, farming and trading with other tribes. The Paiutes were more likely hunter-gatherers, collecting plants and small animals.

When the Paiutes first encountered non-Native Americans is uncertain, but the establishment of the Old Spanish Trail in 1830 forced them into more frequent contact with Europeans. This created both new problems and opportunities for the natives: On one hand, they were among the least warlike of North American native groups, and so they were relatively easy to capture or defeat and enslave. On the other hand, friendly whites introduced new ideas and innovations that were helpful to the tribe. In his travel report, Captain John C. Frémont of the US Army Topographical Corps dismissed the Paiutes as "lizard eaters," drawing attention to the diffi-

Paiute Colony Smoke Shop.

culty with which they sustained themselves in the arid environment. In 1855, however, a group of Mormons settling in the area set up an experimental farm to teach the Paiutes new agricultural techniques—so was born the well-known Kiel Ranch, a historic site that unfortunately has burned.

Paiutes also worked as ranchhands for late nineteenth-century ranch owners Octavius Decatur Gass and Helen J. Stewart. Mrs. Stewart took a great interest in their general welfare, so she gave them 10 acres of land in downtown Las Vegas, just west of Main Street between Owens and Washington. Many of the Las Vegas Paiutes still live there today, some of whom operate a "tribal smoke shop" that offers cigarettes at unusually cheap prices due to different federal regulations governing Native Americans. Northeast of town, between Las Vegas and the Utah line, the Moapa Paiutes live on the Moapa Reservation. The Southern Paiutes of southern Nevada number in the few hundreds today.

Railroad Cottages

As the first decade of the twentieth century came to an end, the San Pedro, Los Angeles, & Salt Lake Railroad (SPLA&SLR) had created the townsite of Las Vegas, and its depot and repair shops provided employment to the town's residents. The next step was to make sure that the railroad workers had a place to live, so the railroad built about 120 houses south of the depot, on South Second, Third, and Fourth Streets, not far from the yards where many of the residents worked. The houses were all made of concrete blocks, with wood frames, a rectangular layout, and a right entrance porch—all typical of the architecture of the time. The railroad built them at a cost of about $1,700 each, and rented them out for up to $20 a month for a four-bedroom house.

The Union Pacific took control of the railroad in 1921, and Las Vegans were strong supporters of the resulting nationwide railroad strike of 1921–22. Once the strike ended, the Union Pacific announced that it would move the Las Vegas repair shops to Caliente, a town north on the railroad line up from Las Vegas, but it vehemently denied that the move was punishment for Las Vegans' support of the strike. Las Vegans would have to find other sources of income, and feared hard times ahead. Since they still had a railroad depot and a desert climate with water available, they looked increasingly to tourism, and eventually turned that unfortunate loss of jobs into an economic blessing.

In the years since, most of the railroad cottages have been torn down to make room for more modern buildings. Several of them remain standing, however, and are even still used as homes or professional offices. Today they are a reminder that the city of Las Vegas largely owes its growth and modern greatness to the railroad that once owned the humble town.

Golden Gate Hotel & Casino

When Las Vegas celebrated its centennial on May 15, 2005, the Golden Gate was turning 99. It opened at the beginning of 1906 as John F. Miller's Hotel Nevada. Miller was a lot like other early Las Vegas businessmen in that he was active in his community. He joined the fight to set up a new county in southern Nevada, and in efforts to build the small town with other early residents. Some of these included Ed W. Clark, who owned part of the power and phone company, a freighting company, a store, and a nearby ranch; Charles P. "Pop" Squires, who owned a tent hotel and, for nearly 40 years, the *Las Vegas Age* newspaper; John S. Park, the cashier for Nevada State Bank at First and Fremont, just a block from Miller's hotel; and Walter Bracken, the local agent for the national railroad and an investor in a water company.

Within the five blocks east of the Hotel Nevada was a variety of businesses and homes. A couple of blocks north was Block 16, which became the local red-light district, where the saloons offered not only illegal alcohol

during Prohibition, but also illegal gambling and prostitutes. The Hotel Nevada was an upstanding place, on the other hand, and offered good value: luxurious rooms for $1 a day. That price suited well the hotel's status as the site of the first telephone in Las Vegas—its phone number was 1.

In 1931, the hotel's name changed to the Sal Sagev (read backwards, it makes perfect sense). So it remained until 1955, when a group of Italian-Americans arrived from San Francisco and opened a casino, the Golden Gate, inside the hotel. One of the new operators, Italo Ghelfi, ran the casino for more than three decades; today one of his sons, Mark Brandenburg, is in charge. The Golden Gate continues to offer its most famous fare: a 99-cent shrimp cocktail, which originally sold for 50 cents when it was introduced in 1959.

The Golden Gate is also the last remaining original structure on the corner where Las Vegas really began. Across the street to the north, the Overland Hotel burned in 1911. It was rebuilt, and today it is the Las Vegas Club. Across the street to the west, the old railroad depot is gone, replaced in 1971 by the Union Plaza Hotel, built by businessman Frank Scott and longtime Las Vegas gaming operators Sam Boyd, Jackie Gaughan, and J. Kell Houssels, Jr. Today, the Plaza still operates under the control of the Barrick Gaming Corporation.

Old Las Vegas: From Railroad Station to Federal Town

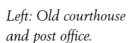
Left: Old courthouse and post office.

Federal Buildings

Downtown Las Vegas is the center of activity for federal offices in Las Vegas, and the histories of the buildings there are interestingly intertwined with some of the city's most famous—law-abiding—personalities. The newest addition to the local federal buildings, the Lloyd George Federal Building, is on Las Vegas Boulevard just south of Bridger, right across from the original Las Vegas townsite. The building is named for a longtime Las Vegas attorney who enjoyed a distinguished career as a federal bankruptcy and district court judge. It includes the offices of the two southern Nevadans who serve on the US Ninth Circuit Court of Appeals, several US district court judges, and other federal officials.

The other two major downtown federal buildings reach farther back in the city's history. Across from the Lloyd George Federal Building is the Foley Federal Building, which houses various federal offices and the bankruptcy court. It is named for the first family of Las Vegas law and politics. Roger T. Foley moved to Las Vegas in 1928, and he and his wife Helen raised five sons here, all of whom followed their father into the practice of law. In 1945, Foley became Nevada's only federal judge, and he continued to hear cases after his official retirement—even almost until his death in 1974. In 1962, after serving as Clark County district attorney and Nevada's attorney general, Roger D. Foley joined his father on the

Pages 42–43: Boat cruise of Lake Mead departing from Las Vegas Boat Harbor.

Lloyd George Federal Building.

federal bench, creating the only father-and-son team of federal judges the United States has ever known. The other sons enjoyed distinguished careers of their own—Tom as a state district judge, Joe as a regent, George as a district attorney, and John as a legislator—and their families have continued the Foley tradition of public service and political activity up into the present.

Before there was a Foley Federal Building, though, Las Vegas had only a single federal building, which doubled as courthouse and post office. Located at Third and Stewart, the building opened in 1933 amid some controversy: before the opening, local officials were supposed to clean up the saloons and brothels on Block 16, just two blocks from where the building was located. That didn't happen, but the building opened on time anyway. (The fate of the brothels on Block 16? Local officials shut them down during World War II for a different reason, but it also involved the federal government: trainees and staff at the nearby army gunnery school were frequenting them a bit too much.) A couple of decades later, the courthouse became the scene of some key

moments in Las Vegas history. In 1950, Senator Estes Kefauver brought his organized-crime investigating committee to the federal building, where he questioned several Strip and downtown casino operators about their mob connections. In 1953, the conspiracy case that *Las Vegas Sun* publisher Hank Greenspun brought against Senator Pat McCarran, his staff, and dozens of local casino operators was tried here. Greenspun accused the group of an illegal conspiracy to deprive his newspaper of advertising revenue as punishment for his criticism of McCarran. The settlement he won struck a blow at McCarran's influence, but the real shocker was the impartial ruling that made that blow possible: Roger T. Foley, the judge presiding over the case, owed his appointment to McCarran, who probably expected preferential treatment as a result.

Today, the city's first federal building is an affiliate of the Smithsonian Institution. It will soon begin hosting museum exhibits and community events as part of downtown redevelopment—an effort whose leaders have included, among others, US District Judge Lloyd George.

Hoover Dam and Lake Mead

The nation's wildest river, the Colorado, often flooded its banks, but in 1905 it flooded so bad that it created the Salton Sea in California's Imperial Valley. Until that time, many had talked of taming its raging waters, but after the flood the talk began in earnest. Finally, in 1921, the seven states that share the Colorado began negotiating the division of its waters, with an eye toward building a dam to bring cheap water and power to the Southwest. Seven years later, the passage of

Las Vegas Boat Harbor, Lake Mead.

Right: Steve Ligouri's High Scaler Monument, Hoover Dam. Sitting in a chair, hundreds of feet high, the high-scaler set charges to clear loose rock from the face of canyon walls.

the Boulder Canyon Project Act enabled the US Bureau of Reclamation to start scouting sites for a dam. The government agency examined about 75 locations in Boulder and Black Canyons before settling on one in the latter.

Construction began in March 1931. The blue-prints called for a massive structure more than 726 feet high, 660 feet wide at the base, and 45 feet wide at the crest—which required more than 3.2 million cubic yards of concrete weighing more than 6.5 million tons to achieve. The creation of the dam simultaneously created the nation's largest man-made lake, named for Elwood Mead, the commissioner of the Bureau of Reclamation at the time of construction.

President Franklin Roosevelt came to dedicate the dam on September 30, 1935, but it was not officially completed until February 29, 1936. The project was actually completed a year early and under budget—but at a terrible price. Over five years, an estimated total 13,000 people worked on the dam, with at least 5,200 working together at the peak of construction. They worked eight-hour shifts around the clock in punishing weather: the sun was unrelenting, and the temperature often topped 120 degrees during the summer, and rose even higher in the tunnels they dug to divert the Colorado. Workers told stories of men falling from the cliffs onto the road and their bodies being left where they fell, because to stop and tend to them would have delayed construction. Those who survived the experience nevertheless took great pride in the results.

Each year, hundreds of thousands of visitors come to marvel at and tour Hoover Dam. Since the terrorist attacks of September 11, 2001, tourists have been unable to go as far into the structure as before, and are no longer permitted to come outside at the bottom of the dam to look up at it. But the Bureau of Reclamation operates a large visitors' center that tells the story of how Hoover Dam was built, and the tour alone is still well worth the trip. Lake Mead has become an attraction in its own right, and it contributes considerably to the beauty and desirability of many local residential communities.

To clear up a frequently asked question, the official name of the structure is in fact Hoover Dam. During his visit to the construction site on September 17, 1930, Secretary of the Interior Ray Lyman Wilbur announced that the dam would be named for his boss, Herbert Hoover. Hoover had indeed played an important role in the project, first as secretary of commerce and then as president. The decision proved unpopular with the workers, however, who had sought work on the dam project because the Great Depression had cost them jobs elsewhere—a plight for which they blamed Hoover. When Franklin Roosevelt took office after defeating Hoover, his new secretary of the interior, Harold Ickes, changed the name to Boulder Dam. So it remained until 1947, when Republicans regained control of Congress and restored Hoover's name to the dam. Legally, that is the name today.

As to the other question commonly asked about Hoover Dam: No, nobody is buried within it.

Boulder Dam Hotel is a community center in Boulder City, and now a site on the National Register of Historic Places.

Boulder City

When the federal government announced plans to build Hoover Dam, Las Vegans were eager to reap the benefits. It was expected that the project would require several thousand workers, and locals optimistically hoped that they would all come to live in Las Vegas. That hope was unrealistic for a couple of reasons: First, Las Vegas is about 30 miles from the dam site, and cars and roads back then were a far cry from what they are today. Second, Las Vegas was already famous for the vices it offered to visitors, and federal officials had no desire to expose their construction workers to pleasures that might divert their attention from the job.

So, federal officials built their own city near the dam site. Originally, it was called the Boulder Canyon Federal Reservation, and the Interior Department ran it much as it would run an

Indian reservation—that is, with total control over the inhabitants. The government hired planners to design the town and construction companies to build housing, both small cottages for families and barracks for single men, as well as a company mess hall. Some of the original housing used by dam workers still stands, including cottages that were trucked up from Los Angeles after they hosted international athletes at the 1932 Olympics. City Manager Sims Ely banned alcohol, gambling, and prostitution in the town. That, at least, was good news for Las Vegas: each payday, the highway into town was filled with cars that were filled with men.

The government's Nevada reservation was a lot like a federal version of a company town, just as company towns were becoming common in the coal mining country of Pennsylvania and West

Virginia, and in the copper towns of the mountainous west. The little master-planned community remained a federal reservation until 1960, when the government handed over control to the state of Nevada and the area's inhabitants. The newly independent city became the fourth incorporated city in Clark County, Nevada (the others were Las Vegas, North Las Vegas, and Henderson; Mesquite has since become the fifth).

Sims Ely would no doubt be proud that Boulder City is still the only Nevada city in which gambling is illegal, although casinos are just a quick walk across the city limits. For those who live in the older part of town, restaurants, markets, and shops are a short walk away. The Boulder Dam Hotel, built during the 1930s, is home to much more than rooms: shops, dining, and an interesting museum are enjoyed by

Older houses from the dam-building era, like this one, still dot the Boulder City landscape.

View of Lake Mead from Boulder City.

tourists and locals alike. A couple doors down, the Boulder Theatre hosts an assortment of programs, including a Chautauqua early each September. Modeled on the old tent shows that originated in the nineteenth century in the New York town of the same name, the Boulder City Chautauqua features nationally renowned scholars who have carefully studied historical figures in order to be able to depict them accurately in their performances.

Boulder City residents of today pride themselves on maintaining a small-town lifestyle amid the bustle of a resort mecca. They deliberately limit growth so that the population remains small—currently it's a little more than 15,000. Drivers need deal with only two traffic lights, both of which are on the highway leading from Las Vegas to the dam. The downside of this small-town atmosphere for Boulder City residents is that property is more expensive there than in many parts of nearby Las Vegas. And—rather ironically, when one considers the town's concerted efforts to limit growth—some of Boulder City's residents hardly spend any time there. They are not Nevada residents, but Californians and "snowbirds" from colder climates who buy homes there in order to take advantage of Nevada's lack of income and estate taxes. Then again, maybe they're just there to enjoy the spectacular lake views.

Nevada Test Site

The Nevada Test Site was both a boon to Las Vegas and a warning to the nation. In the early 1950s, the federal government began searching for a domestic site for atomic testing. The location inland was due mainly to security considerations, but the government also recognized that a test site near an urban area would have better access to the services a city already provided, from transportation and residences for workers to utilities for the site itself. Late in 1950, President Harry Truman approved the creation of the Atomic Proving Ground about 65 miles northwest of Las Vegas. The first atomic test was performed on January 28, 1951. Over the next twelve years, the Atomic Energy Commission detonated about 120 aboveground atomic bombs, each one sending up a formidable mushroom cloud from the desert wasteland. After the US–Soviet Test Ban Treaty of 1963, the tests went underground. By the time nuclear testing finally ended in 1992, hundreds of additional tests had been carried out below the Nevada Test Site.

At the time, the underground tests attracted protesters and led to claims from test site workers that they had suffered exposure to radiation. It is actually the aboveground tests, however, that remain the most controversial atomic tests to this day. They are perhaps *the* icon of 1950s Cold War culture, and a particularly potent symbol for Las Vegas. Thanks to the many

Line-of-sight pipes are fabricated inside tunnels at Rainier Mesa on DOE's Nevada Test Site.

reports in the 1950s that the mob controlled Las Vegas casinos and prostitution, many Americans of that era already saw Nevada as their nation's central clearinghouse for vice. The tests enabled Nevadans to counteract that reputation a bit by doing the patriotic duty of hosting a major defense project (in addition to the half-dozen military installations already scattered around the state). Locals also welcomed the millions of research dollars and payrolls that the military presence created.

The great mushroom clouds also benefited the state in other ways—ways that probably nobody could have expected. Media from around the world came to southern Nevada to ooh and aah at the aboveground atomic blasts. Gamblers began leaving the tables to watch the clouds shoot up into the sky, then quickly returned to their games. Las Vegans took advantage of the opportunity to market the mushroom cloud as a tourist attraction: the Atomic View Motel offered guests folding chairs on the roof for a good view of the action, a local salon offered an atomic hairdo, bars made atomic cocktails—purporting that the mix of liquors created the same effect as an atomic blast in the head—club-goers danced to the "Atomic Boogie" and the "Atomic Bomb Bounce," and there was, of course, a Miss Atomic Blast beauty contest. Nevada postcards, county seals, and school yearbooks of the day all featured mushroom clouds, the great symbol of American military and technological might.

Songs and films from across the country contributed to the fun attention the bombs received, but they rarely acknowledged the darker side of the tests that locals quickly became aware of. When desert winds blew the mushroom clouds away from the test site, sheep around nearby St. George, Utah

Sedan Crater was formed when a 100-kiliton explosive buried under 635 feet of desert alluvium was fired at the Nevada Test Site on July 6, 1962, displacing 12 million tons of earth. The crater is 320 feet deep and 1,280 feet in diameter.

Small herds of wild horses roam the high elevations of the Nevada Test Site.

mysteriously died. Almost everyone filming *The Conqueror* in the vicinity of the test site was later diagnosed with cancer. Test site workers often suffered from cancer and other illnesses that they accused the government of causing by exposing them to radiation. What the government actually knew and at which stage it realized it remain controversial questions. Federal officials have yet to admit completely to the unhealthful effects of atomic testing—in part because the ensuing lawsuits from those affected would undoubtedly cost the nation millions.

The location of the atomic test site in Nevada has had other effects on the state as well. Many in the US increasingly distrusted the federal government in the wake of the Vietnam War and political scandals such as Watergate, but the local problems from the test site especially intensified Nevadans' desire that the federal government leave them alone. Nevertheless, when Congress and the Ronald Reagan administration first began eyeing Yucca Mountain, located on the Nevada Test Site, as the site of the nation's first high-level nuclear waste repository in 1983, Nevadans welcomed the project. Reagan was popular in Nevada, and not many had yet grasped the effects of the earlier testing. As more information came out and the Cold War ended, however, Nevadans and their political leaders increasingly opposed the proposed dump. The facility has been under construction for nearly 20 years now, and locals continue to fight the project to this day—more than two decades after the dump was first proposed, and more than half a century after the first atomic test.

McCarran International Airport

The first thing people notice about McCarran International Airport is something quite unusual for international airports: the clang of coins entering (and occasionally exiting) slot machines greets—and tempts—waiting passengers. That's all too usual for Las Vegas and the airport actually has much more interesting features than its gambling opportunities. Its name is historically significant to Nevada and, indeed, to the nation. Born and raised near Reno, Pat McCarran became Nevada's first native-born US senator in 1932.

McCarran became a major force in both Nevada and Washington, DC. He was a true believer in Communist conspiracies and infiltration, and he won national attention for his anti-Communist crusade. He was a controversial figure, though, and many claimed he trampled individual rights in his quest to hunt down Communists. Particularly in Nevada, the name McCarran evoked mixed emotions: On the one hand, he helped thousands of Nevadans with personal problems, obtained patronage jobs for about 50 young Nevadans that put them through law and other professional schools, and he succeeded in winning a series of contracts for military bases and defense projects that brought the state a continuous supply of jobs and federal money. On the other hand, he seemed to want to run the state single-handedly and was known for manipulating officeholders, hence his administration tended to create a general climate of fear and corruption in spite of its success.

The fact that Las Vegas named an airport for the man is no coincidence. As a US senator, McCarran contributed greatly to the creation of the Civil Aeronautics Board (a precursor to the Federal Aviation Administration), to the development of aviation in southern Nevada, and he personally negotiated the 1941 landswap that moved the city's airfield to its current site—and got his name put on it. When jets began arriving at McCarran Field in the early 1960s, it was a major step in the development of Las Vegas' tourist industry. McCarran has since evolved into

Slot machines at McCarran International Airport.

an international airport with four major terminals and hundreds of daily national and international flights. It is the nation's sixth busiest airport, and it is constantly expanding.

The airport has also affected the valley's development. An airfield at this site made perfect sense to those who chose it, because they never expected Las Vegas to grow so much. But housing now surrounds the airport, and federal and local officials have teamed up to alleviate ever-worsening traffic congestion by expanding southern Nevada's freeway system with a beltway circling the valley. The beltway runs just east of the airport and provides commuters with easy access to McCarran. The beltway's construction, like the airport's almost constant expansion itself, is a tribute to the city's great engineers and planners, and to the great importance of this airport that serves a significant portion of visitors to Las Vegas—nearly 40 million in 2004.

DESERT PASSAGE

The Old Strip: From Siegel to Caesars

Previous page: Aladdin Resort & Casino.

Caesars Palace

Jay Sarno is the man who helped inspire the modern Las Vegas boom—without ever spending or making a dime on it. When he came to town, there were already several hotels in Las Vegas modeled on places like Morocco or the Caribbean, but Sarno envisioned something new: a *true* theme-resort.

When Caesars Palace opened in 1966 at a cost of $24 million—more than twice the original projected amount—it was everything Sarno had dreamed of, and nothing like anything Las Vegas had ever seen. Several characteristics made the Palace stand out: First, instead of writing the word "Caesar's," with an apostrophe, as one would expect to see it, Sarno intentionally left the apostrophe out. The apostrophe would mean that the palace belongs to just Emperor Julius himself; Sarno reasoned that, at his resort,

"Caesars" really refers to all his guests—every one of them should feel like a Roman conqueror in his palace. Second, he wanted the resort built as a series of ovals, because he believed that the shape was relaxing. The result is a casino that functions like the hub of a wheel, from which the establishment's other attractions jut outward like spokes. Third, he set the resort far back from the street, an arrangement that gave him the opportunity to construct a glorious 135-foot driveway lined with eighteen large fountains and imported Italian cypresses.

And finally, there was the totally complete theme of ancient Rome. The tons of stone and marble used to construct the building were actually imported from Italy. The staff wore togas and tunics. In the middle of the casino a floating, ship-shaped platform called Cleopatra's Barge served as the lounge. Frank Sinatra was welcomed at the 800-seat Circus Maximus Theater, modeled on the Colosseum in Rome. The swimming pool was shaped like a Roman shield. The Bacchanal Room offered gourmet meals with a distinctively Roman flavor. Even the stationery looked like Roman parchment. Jo Harris, who worked as Sarno's designer, explained this near-obsessive authenticity: "I believe very strongly that when you select a theme for a hotel, you ought to follow that theme in every aspect of the operation where it is possible to do so." Looking at Caesars, nobody could ever call Harris a hypocrite, and it was her integrity that set the standard for all the theme-resorts that were to follow.

Caesars was an instant hit. The $1 million, three-day-long opening party headlined by singer Andy Williams offered its guests what was then the largest order of Alaskan king crab and Ukrainian caviar ever requested, 50,000 glasses of champagne, and two tons of filet mignon. Sarno even had to borrow additional money from the Teamsters to cover the winnings by high-rollers because he refused to limit their bets.

While Caesars today is technically defined as part of the "old" Strip, it has had no trouble keeping up with the newcomers. In 1992, it added the Forum Shoppes, which took shopping to a new level in Las Vegas hotels, helping prompt a building boom and huge profits in that sector of the industry. An addition to the Forum Shoppes in 1997 brought Las Vegas its first caviar restaurant and a show about Atlantis—complete with fire, of course. As part of Caesars World, then as the flagship hotel-casino of Caesars Entertainment, Caesars continued to add towers and attractions. In 2003 it took the biggest step in Las Vegas entertainment in recent years when it built the 4,000-seat Colosseum for Canadian pop diva Celine Dion. When she's away, Elton John performs his own glitzy show there.

Caesars Palace Roman Plaza.

The Frontier Hotel, the oldest property on the strip.

The Frontier Hotel and Casino

The Frontier got its start back when the Strip was still just a dream. Its origins go back to 1930 and the opening of the Pair-O-Dice south of Las Vegas on Highway 91, the road to Los Angeles. Since then, however, the Frontier has had many, many faces. Different names have included the 91 Club, Hotel Last Frontier, and New Frontier. Renovations and rebuilding have created a multitude of images, from a Wild West motif to a tribute to the solar system. And particularly interesting is the hotel-casino's series of owners, from Guy McAfee, a former Los Angeles policeman, to Maury Friedman, who eventually went to jail for cheating at cards in a southern Californian Friar's Club.

Then, in 1967, Howard Hughes added the hotel to his expanding empire, and a bit of stability was finally experienced at the Frontier. Hughes was hardly the most normal of the hotel's long list of owners, though: living

across the street in the Desert Inn penthouse, he communicated with his staff through memos, stayed up all night watching movies, and apparently let his hair and fingernails grow to great lengths while planning a virtual takeover of Las Vegas. Hughes' company ran the hotel for nearly a quarter of a century, but businessman Phil Ruffin has been owner since 1997. Ruffin has announced plans to tear down the hotel and replace it with City-by-the-Bay, a San Francisco-themed resort.

The Frontier also has two major claims to fame: First, in 1954, its showroom was the scene of an act starring a then-minor Hollywood actor named Ronald Reagan, whose two-week stay included singing, dancing, and cavorting with chimps. Shortly thereafter, Reagan became host of the television series *Death Valley Days*, and not long after that broke into the world of politics. Just two years after Reagan monkeyed around there, the Frontier booked a particular entertainer for his very first Las Vegas performance: Elvis Presley. He bombed that time, but as everybody knows, he would come back with a vengeance—just like Reagan and Las Vegas, albeit in *very* different ways.

Bally's

Opened as Bonanza Hotel and Casino in 1967, this wildly popular establishment would eventually become Bally's, but with every year the venture actually became more and more of a true bonanza. Its ultimate success had less to do with its origins, though, and more to do with one of the most important figures in modern Las Vegas, Kirk Kerkorian, who bought the Bonanza in the early 1970s. He soon announced plans to tear down the Bonanza and build in its place something truly spectacular: a hotel modeled on the 1932 MGM film *Grand Hotel*.

On December 5, 1973, Cary Grant and Raquel Welch cut the ribbon—made of celluloid to signify the hotel's connection to the film world—that opened the MGM Grand. Dean Martin, who later gave one of his last performances on the same stage, entertained the hotel-casino's very first visitors inside. For $107 million, Kerkorian had gotten 26 stories, 2,084 hotel rooms, and a 1,200-seat showroom, qualifying the building as the world's new largest hotel, just like Kerkorian's International at its opening. Distinguishing the MGM Grand even more were an eight-lane porte cochere that marked the entry to the property, a jai alai arena, and a movie theater that showed classic MGM films and featured couches for extra viewing comfort—a touch that many Las Vegans who frequented the theater in the 1970s and '80s still recall fondly.

The Grand was a grand success, but tragedy marred its happy history on the morning of November 21, 1980. A tiny electrical short broke out into a 2,400-degree fire that roared through the casino and restaurants and out the hotel's main entrance. The interior was completely gutted, but what was worse, more than 80 people were killed and about 1,000 were

injured. Some expected Kerkorian simply to give up, but eight months later, the MGM Grand reopened with a new $5 million fire safety system, once again setting the standard for Las Vegas. The newly opened hotel also featured a new show, veteran Las Vegas producer and choreographer Donn Arden's "Jubilee," which still manages to draw throngs today.

In 1986, Kerkorian sold his Las Vegas and Reno MGM Grands to Bally Manufacturing for $594 million. Bally put its name on the hotel, but it has since become part of Caesars Entertainment. No matter what they call it, the hotel-casino remains truly Grand.

Flamingo

The history of the Flamingo is central to Las Vegas myth and reality. Construction started in 1945 under the ownership of Billy Wilkerson, a Hollywood businessman and publisher who wanted a hangout for his show business friends. However, Wilkerson seemed to have a silent partner from the very beginning. After a series of problems during construction, that partner finally broke his silence . . .

Benjamin Siegel earned the nickname Bugsy—which he hated—for his violent, crazy temper. He grew up in New York City, where he formed the Bug and Meyer Mob with his old friend Meyer Lansky. In the mid-1930s, he moved to California, partly to handle east coast organized crime operations there, partly hoping to become a movie star. In the early 1940s, he and Lansky started making plans for Las Vegas ventures. Just to get started, they had partners of theirs purchase the El Cortez, a downtown casino. But Siegel, like Wilkerson, wanted to impress his Hollywood friends, and the El Cortez was not going to suffice.

The Flamingo, however, was a bit too much: construction topped the then-astronomical sum of $6 million, way over Siegel's budget, and one of his many girlfriends, Virginia Hill, apparently stole a million. Opening night was not well planned, either: The week between Christmas and New Year's used to be one of the worst of the year for Las Vegas, and Siegel opened the Flamingo on December 26. In 1946, that also happened to be the night of a terrible rainstorm, which kept away even more would-be guests. More bad planning prevented Siegel from completing the hotel by the opening date, so most of the guests who did come wound up spending more money to sleep someplace else—not a good first impression.

The property closed shortly thereafter and reopened March 1, at which time it started to recoup its losses. It was too late for Siegel, though: his spending habits and increasingly wild temperament annoyed his associates, and in June 1947 a gunman shot him to death in his girlfriend's Beverly Hills bungalow. Within minutes after the news arrived in Las Vegas, the Flamingo already had new managers—whom Lansky's biographer likened to "generals mopping up after a coup." The new big boss was Gus Greenbaum, a bookmaker from Phoenix with experience in the gambling business. The first year Greenbaum was at the controls, the Flamingo reported a $4 million profit, assuring its success in the future.

The Flamingo has changed hands many times since then. It became the first of Kirk Kerkorian's many Las Vegas hotel-casinos, and it was the most profitable hotel in the entire Hilton chain for a while. Most of Bugsy's personal touches have been eliminated today—including his secret escape routes from police and unhappy mob associates—but he would undoubtedly be pleased with the hangout today.

Sahara Hotel and Casino

The Sahara's ancestry can be traced to Butte, Montana and Portland, Oregon—unlikely places for a casino. Neither was a stranger to illegal gambling in the 1940s, though, and they're the places the Sahara's original owners began their careers. In October 1952, Montanan Milton Prell and Oregonian Al Winter opened the Arabian-nights-themed Sahara, with rooms like the Congo Room and Casbar Lounge.

Like the other Strip hotel-casinos of the 1950s, the Sahara boasted big-name entertainment, but it became better known for the quality of its showroom and lounge performers. Opening night starred song-and-dance man Ray Bolger, the scarecrow from *The Wizard of Oz*. From then on, Louis Prima and Keely Smith, with Sam Butera and the Witnesses, made entertainment history nightly, setting a standard for Las Vegas lounges. Don Rickles made his Las Vegas debut at the Sahara, insulting and convulsing audience members. Later, Johnny

Carson frequented the Sahara, bringing the hotel additional publicity by mentioning his coming appearances there on *The Tonight Show*.

Entertainment was not lacking off-stage, either. In 1961, the hotel-casino hosted the PGA Tournament of Champions, and even brought some of the New York Yankees' star players to appear at the event. Then, in 1964, the swarming crowds of young ladies in love made for fabulous entertainment out in front of the hotel: The

Beatles, scheduled to perform at the Convention Center up the street, were staying at the Sahara.

The hotel changed hands several times in the coming decades. Seemingly regardless of owner, it prospered for most of its history. But by the time William Bennett took over in the mid-1990s, the Sahara was suffering. In addition to sorely needing renovation, its location was no longer prime picking: most of the major construction of the late 1980s and '90s went on at the southern end of the Strip, while the Sahara is far north on the four neon miles. To make up for that, Bennett decided to take advantage of the nationally growing popularity of NASCAR. He got involved in building the Las Vegas Motor Speedway north of town, and the Sahara became a favorite hotel for stock-car racing fans. That seems to have attracted new construction north, and since then things have only gotten better for the Sahara.

The Riviera Hotel & Casino

The Riviera was the Strip's very first high-rise, and it still towers above the Strip today. The original ownership group included several operators tied to Meyer Lansky—and both Gummo and Harpo Marx. The 11-story, $10 million hotel-casino opened with a splash on April 20, 1955. Joan Crawford served as hostess, and the showroom headliner was Liberace, who received a then-whopping $50,000 a week for his performances.

Within three months, however, the Riviera was about to close due to steep financial losses.

Signs advertising the Riviera's wide selection of games.

There were two causes: First, five new Las Vegas resorts opened in 1955, suddenly overwhelming the market. Second, some of the Riviera's operators reportedly got their positions solely because of their ties to Chicago kingpin Sam Giancana, not because they actually knew anything about the gambling business.

But the Riviera would not go under entirely. Gus Greenbaum, who had plans to retire back in Phoenix, gave in to pressure from some with hidden interests in the Riviera and stayed to save it. (Greenbaum had no desire to stay whatsoever, but their "persuasion" allegedly involved murdering his sister-in-law.) By 1958, Greenbaum's knowledge of what went on behind the scenes, combined with a worsening drug addiction, led to his and his wife's murder in their Arizona home. The case remains unsolved, but it is known that several Chicago gangland leaders happened to be visiting Arizona at the time.

Until 1973, the Riviera continued to prosper in the hands of gaming industry veterans. Then the hotel-casino was sold to Meshulam Riklis, a brokerage analyst who had risen to stardom as one of Wall Street's leading leveraging and takeover artists. He refurbished the hotel and its convention area, but by the early 1990s, the Riviera found itself in bankruptcy court—again. This time, Riviera Holdings Corporation (RHC) would save the establishment's tail, but rumors that the Riviera will be sold persist even after a decade of stability.

Stardust Resort and Casino

Just to clear the air up front: the film *Casino* was *based on* fact, but it was still a fictional version of what went on at the Stardust. There is much more to the Stardust's story than director Martin Scorsese's and writer Nicholas Pileggi's vision of it. The hotel was the brainchild of Tony Cornero, who built the first "carpet joint"—casino with carpeting on the floor—in Las Vegas after legalization of wide-open gambling in 1931. He then returned to Southern California, where he was involved in illegal gambling and bootlegging. During construction of the Stardust in 1955, he ran into trouble: not only did he fail to file the legally required paperwork, but he sold more stock in the hotel than actually existed. While consoling himself one night at one of his favorite pastimes—shooting craps at the Desert Inn—Cornero died of a heart attack.

Chicago-based interests took over ownership, in tandem with the group that built the Desert Inn. That was good news: The Desert Inn's builders—onetime rumrunners and illegal casino operators known in Cleveland as the Mayfield Road Gang—were among the Strip's most respected and astute businessmen. With them at the controls, the Stardust that opened on July 2, 1958 was much more than the one Cornero had seen in his dreams. Its more than 1,000-room hotel, 16,500-square-foot casino, and 105-foot-long swimming pool were all by far the largest on the Strip. The owners later added a horseman's park and rodeo facility, a grand prix auto-racing track, and a golf course. Indoor entertainment included one of the most important, elaborate production shows in Las Vegas history: the Lido de Paris, complete with beautiful showgirls, specialty acts such as magicians and acrobats, and no less than the sinking of the Titanic. And to make the Stardust all the easier to find, a helpful sign was installed: it measured 216 feet long and 27 feet high, and included six miles of wiring, 7,100 feet of neon tubing, and 11,000 lamps.

As much as they were a blessing in the beginning, its ties to Chicago proved to be a problem for the Stardust in the end. In the early 1970s, the Teamsters Central States Pension Fund—a longtime cash cow for Las Vegas casino operators who had trouble getting legitimate funding elsewhere—loaned southern California developer Allen Glick $62.7 million to buy the Stardust, Fremont, and Hacienda hotels. Glick proved to be the front man for Chicago, Kansas City, and Milwaukee organized-crime interests, but, more importantly, he also proved not to be the Stardust's real owner, as everybody presumed. The real boss was Frank Rosenthal, a veteran of illegal betting and gambling with ties to organized-crime figures in Chicago. A longtime bookmaker, Rosenthal introduced a key innovation to the Las Vegas sports betting scene: a large race and sports book inside the Stardust casino itself.

When federal and state investigations and

newspaper reports accused Stardust executives of skimming millions for the mob, Rosenthal was unable to obtain a state license to remain an executive at the hotel. He engaged in a fiery confrontation with state gaming officials that earned him the nickname "Crazy" in the underworld, and he came very near death when someone blew up his car, apparently because mobsters feared he was about to testify against them. But he did live . . . to tell his story through *Casino*. In the movie, Robert DeNiro played Ace Rothstein, the character modeled on Rosenthal. (An Italian actor playing a Jewish mobster does a lot to explain the image of organized crime in America. Many tend to see all mobsters as Italian, which obviously is untrue.) Sharon Stone portrayed a woman who was supposed to resemble Rosenthal's beautiful, troubled wife, Geri. And Joe Pesci was a caricature of the Chicago mob's muscleman in Las Vegas, Tony Spilotro, whose story probably is the most accurate part of the film.

Glick eventually had to give up his casinos. At the Stardust, Al Sachs, a respected, longtime Las Vegas casino executive took over. Even under new ownership, though, the Stardust remained in the grip of Chicago mob figures who kept skimming money. State officials revoked Sachs' license in 1983, four years after he had bought out Glick, and asked Boyd Gaming to manage the operation. Boyd did so, then went on to buy the hotel, which it still owns today.

While the Stardust is no longer part of the organized crime system that so many think of when they hear the words Las Vegas, it does still enjoy several ties to the old Strip. Wayne Newton, for example, who has performed in Las Vegas since 1959, when he was booked as a teenager in the Fremont lounge downtown, appeared exclusively at the Stardust for several years. He's gone now, but such Las Vegas icons as Don Rickles, Steve Lawrence, and Eydie Gorme still play there—hardly a disappointment for guests.

Aladdin Resort & Casino

The Aladdin Hotel has a checkered history of controversy and trouble that extends back well beyond the hotel one sees today. The original hotel was built by the inventor of Yahtzee, who thought that a Las Vegas hotel could succeed without a casino. He was wrong, and so Milton Prell bought the hotel and turned it into the Arabian Nights-themed Aladdin. The addition of gambling and big-name entertainment brightened the hotel's future, but the establishment's real moment in the sun was on May 1, 1967, when Elvis married Priscilla there.

As most people know, that marriage proved ill-fated—and so did the Aladdin. Illness forced Prell to sell the hotel, and in 1979 federal prosecutors briefly closed the casino after it was discovered to have ties to organized crime. Then came a particularly ugly public battle between Johnny Carson and Wayne Newton over who would buy it. Newton won that battle, but he was less successful as casino owner, and he eventually sold his interest to his more experienced business partner. The Aladdin still wound up in chapter 11 bankruptcy, and it had to close again for more than a year until new owners could be found. The casino never recovered from that closure, and for a while the only success the Aladdin enjoyed came from the big concerts at the Aladdin Theater.

In 2000, developer Jack Sommer knocked down the old hotel—probably trying to get rid of its curse—and opened his much larger, much fancier $1 billion-plus resort on the same spot. Unfortunately, between management problems and a fall-off in business after the terrorist attacks of September 11, 2001, this Aladdin met a fate similar to that of its predecessor when it filed for chapter 11 bankruptcy protection. Now with Planet Hollywood and the Sheraton at the wheel, the Aladdin continues to offer concerts, shopping, and gambling as usual, still trying to overcome the hex that has dogged the property since the beginning.

Circus Circus Hotel-Casino

The big top at the Circus Circus helped build modern Las Vegas. It was another brainchild of Caesars Palace creator Jay Sarno, who originally thought of using the Roman theme again. But when the Circus Circus opened on October 17, 1968, it turned out to be unique. Sarno dressed like a big-top ringmaster (which he was, in a sense) and the 200 invited guests wore tuxedoes and evening gowns—but discovered when they arrived that they had to slide down a giant metal slide in order to enter the basement casino.

The Circus Circus started as only a casino beneath a four-story concrete tent, but it was a casino like no other: trapeze artists, mimes, and clowns swung above, carnival barkers touted sideshows, and the ringmaster held an hourly auction.

Different as it seemed, the Circus Circus did not mark a change in how Las Vegas tried to reach tourists—at least, not yet. It was certainly not designed for children, but, as one critic said, "for adults who wanted to act like kids." The

Circus Circus' marquee.

Ooh-La-La Theater featured topless showgirls, and the casino displayed a nude, supposedly prehistoric woman in a block of ice. Sarno's innovations aimed at distinguishing the casino actually caused it to lose money: he prohibited children from entering, charged admission for adults, and refused to install safety nets for the trapeze artists—even after one of them landed on a craps table in the middle of big-action betting, sending chips flying all over the casino. The casino's gaudiness appalled many, as well, even Hunter S. Thompson (the man on whose life the film *Fear and Loathing in Las Vegas* was based), who was pretty hard to appall. He wrote one famous criticism of the casino: "Circus Circus is what the whole hep world would be doing on Saturday night if the Nazis had won the war."

What was worse, the lack of a hotel kept high-rollers from visiting the casino. This prompted Sarno to obtain another Teamsters loan, just as he had for Caesars, but this time at a price: the head of the pension fund, Allen Dorfman, was tied to Chicago organized crime interests and asked Sarno to give a gift shop concession to a Chicago businessman in return for the loan. That "businessman" turned out to be Tony Spilotro, the street boss who inspired Joe Pesci's character in the film *Casino*. Completing the hotel did help matters, but the Circus Circus still continued to lose money until Sarno sold it in 1974.

That led to changes that ultimately revolutionized Las Vegas. The new owners were William Bennett, who had worked for the Del Webb Corporation at the downtown Mint Hotel-Casino, and William Pennington, who had achieved great success with early models of blackjack video machines. Bennett and Pennington separated the circus acts and games from the casino, welcomed parents who came to gamble while their children enjoyed the carnival games, and, most importantly of all, marketed the Circus Circus to middle-class vacationers, with low room rates and lower betting limits. As

Bennett once reasoned aloud: "There are a hell of a lot more working stiffs out there than high-rollers." The new casino emphasized slot machines, which most operators then considered just a sideline to occupy wives while their husbands shot craps. When Michael Milken—who eventually went to jail for insider-trading at Drexel Burnham Lambert—finally helped Bennett and Pennington take their company onto Wall Street, it became fabulously profitable.

Accordingly, the company grew. It added other local properties and built hotel-casinos in Reno and Laughlin. Bennett hired a corps of outstanding young executives headed by Glenn Schaeffer and Mike Ensign to lead the company into the twenty-first century. But in the late 1980s and early 1990s, as the company added new Strip resorts like the Excalibur and the Luxor, Bennett began forcing out his top aides in order to play a larger role in running the company himself—and stock prices fell. When Bennett's newly hired president, Clyde Turner, proposed selling the Circus Circus, the board of directors finally forced out Bennett. The company kept its old big top and continued to grow, eventually changing its name to Mandalay Resorts—a name that would become closely associated with the evolution of the new Strip.

The New Strip: Megaresorts, Mergers, and Money

The Mirage's trademark volcano in full eruption.

The Mirage

Steve Wynn opened the Mirage hotel on November 22, 1989—and that opening marks the start of the modern Las Vegas boom. A few years before, Wynn had informed other hotel operators that they needed to expand their casino facilities, to do everything bigger and better. The Mirage was the project he undertook to show them just what he meant. And with 3,044 rooms built at a cost of $630 million, he *really* showed them.

Many thought that Wynn even went too far. He signed Siegfried & Roy to a long-term contract, built a theater for them, installed a habitat for their white tigers, another one for dolphins, and built Siegfried & Roy's Secret Garden for the two illusionists' many feline friends. He charged nearly $100 per show to see them, and they sold out every night. He filled a three-acre lagoon in front of the hotel with water and built a 50-foot-high volcano that erupted every 15 minutes throughout the evening. Pedestrians gathered outside the hotel to watch, then somehow found their way inside. To create the Mirage's Polynesian rain forest theme, Wynn built a 90-foot-high atrium at the reception desk, complete with a misting system,

Pages 78–79: View of the Strip and the MGM Grand.

The Mirage's pool—complete with waterfall.

a 20,000-gallon aquarium, and 90 species of tropical fish.

The Mirage was the foundation on which Wynn built his Strip empire, which proved so successful that Kirk Kerkorian's MGM bought him out in 2000. Today, the Mirage remains a Las Vegas hotspot—and not just because of the volcano.

The atrium at the reception desk reflects the Mirage's Polynesian rain forest theme.

Treasure Island

Treasure Island was made for everyone who ever dreamed of growing up to be a pirate. Steve Wynn opened the resort on October 27, 1993, at the exact moment that he blew up the Dunes—a spectacle he aired live on television. Ever since then, the pirates have been firing away right beside the Mirage, on the corner of Spring Mountain Road and the Strip. The $450 million hotel boasts 2,885 rooms in three 36-floor towers, and as of June 2005 a pedestrian bridge will connect the establishment to the Fashion Show Mall across the street.

Originally, the Treasure Island was best known for its nightly outdoor pirate show, in which pirates would attack a British ship on the lagoon in front of the resort. Every 90 minutes, shots would ring out across the lagoon and people would gather on the wooden planks around it to

"Sirens of TI," the outdoor show at Treasure Island that pits pirates against their siren foes.

watch the show—then accept the sea captain's invitation to come into the resort. One actor did all of the voices for the show, except—according to rumor—for one, which is supposedly Wynn's very own. After MGM bought out Wynn, the new owners began calling the resort "TI" and changed the show to "Sirens of TI," with the marauding pirates now meeting their match in the form of beautiful women. They also brought the show to the internet, meaning that it can now be seen in places where pirates actually roamed.

The TI's main entertainment—aside from the sirens and pirates—is Mystère, performed in a 1,600-seat theater by 70 acrobats, actors, clowns, comedians, and musicians. The latest addition at the TI is the Tangerine Lounge and Nightclub, which features an outdoor deck, rock music, and a burlesque revue—all part of the resort's evolving efforts to reach younger adult audiences.

MGM Grand

On December 18, 1993, Kirk Kerkorian opened the new MGM Grand on the Marina lot at Tropicana and Las Vegas Boulevard South. The Marina had been a small property; Kerkorian, on the other hand, had already won distinction as builder of the world's largest hotel—twice. His new MGM Grand would earn him that title for a third time.

Kerkorian was born in Fresno, California in 1917. He quit school in the eighth grade to become a boxer, served as a pilot in World War II, then started his own airline. He started gambling in Las Vegas in the 1940s, betting thousands at the craps tables. He invested his money in land and eventually wound up with several Las Vegas resorts. In 1973, he built the original MGM Grand, but the new MGM Grand is his real crowning achievement—so far.

The $1 billion hotel boasts 5,034 guest rooms, 751 suites, four 30-story towers, 29

private villas at the Mansion at MGM Grand, more than 170,000 square feet of gambling, 5 outdoor pools, and a 100,000-pound, 45-foot-tall bronze statue of a lion that greets visitors at the hotel entrance. Behind that is a $100 million, 380,000-square-foot conference center. The MGM Grand Garden Arena has hosted concerts by such outstanding stars as the Rolling Stones, Paul McCartney, Bette Midler, and Barbra Streisand. The hotel offers a variety of other entertainment as well: KÁ, a Cirque du Soleil show that features a group of 72 artists performing acrobatic feats and using a variety of multimedia in a 1,950-seat arena; headliners from Tom Jones to David Copperfield, all performing at the hotel's Hollywood Theater;

and of course, Studio 54, modeled on the famous New York City nightclub of the 1970s. The Lion Habitat, located just a few miles from the MGM Grand, offers tours that allow visitors to walk above and below the cats that have been the symbol of MGM since the 1930s. Within "the city of entertainment," as the MGM Grand is known, are restaurants run by celebrity chefs such as Wolfgang Puck, Emeril Lagasse, and Michael Mina.

In 2005, MGM Mirage, the resort's parent company, merged with Mandalay Resort Group. The new company continues to make grand plans for future development, and guarantees that the lions at MGM will continue to roar for a long time to come.

New York–New York Hotel & Casino

New York City is known by many names: the Big Apple, the city that never sleeps, the town so nice they named it twice—and many other less favorable monikers as well. The Las Vegas version of New York, New York offers all the fun of New York without any of those less favorable aspects. The 2,023-room hotel opened January 3, 1997 as the result of a partnership between MGM Grand's Kirk Kerkorian and Gary Primm, who built the town on the California-Nevada border that bears his name. What they erected is not exactly the Big City, but it comes close in several ways: Numerous

skyscrapers modeled on the Empire State Building, the Seagram's Building, the Chrysler Building, and other New York landmarks tower over the Strip. A collection of landmarks features a 150-foot replica of the Statue of Liberty and a 300-foot-long, 50-foot-high replica of the Brooklyn Bridge, along with such attractions as the terminal at Grand Central Station, the United Nations building, and the reception area at Ellis Island. The complex also boasts an authentic branch of that most distinctive of New York restaurants: Nathan's Hot Dogs.

The entertainment at New York–New York is

as diverse as the city for which it is named: from Zumanity, the most erotic of the Cirque du Soleil shows, to Rita Rudner, the comedienne-talk show host who resides and is active in the Las Vegas community. The Manhattan Express Roller Coaster that encircles the complex peaks at 203 feet and at one point drops 144 feet, and reaches a maximum speed of 67 miles per hour—almost as fast as some of the real New York City's cab drivers. The Coney Island Emporium is a 32,000-square-foot entertainment center with a plethora of arcade games, from video games to bowling. Even the casino continues the theme: there are sections evoking Park Avenue, Times Square, Greenwich Village, and the Financial District (Wall Street and Las Vegas are obviously very important to one another). Understandably, the most ornate bathroom facility in the whole casino is called the Rockefeller Restroom.

In 2001, New York–New York was the scene of one of the more unusual memorials to take place in Las Vegas—or anywhere else in the country,

for that matter. After the terrorist attacks of September 11, Las Vegans and tourists from around the world created their own memorial at the base of the Statue of Liberty. They deposited there memorabilia similar to that placed around Ground Zero in the wake of that terrible day: mementos from police and fire stations, flowers, flags, and poems. The University of North Las Vegas' gaming research director, David Schwartz, curates the collection today.

New York–New York's downstairs bar, "Nine Fine Irishmen."

Wynn Las Vegas

Steve Wynn advertised his new hotel as so special that he was willing to put his name on it. For locals, it's special for a very particular reason: it sits on the site of one of Las Vegas' historic hotels, the venerable Desert Inn. Although it was truly a local landmark and pop culture icon, the Desert Inn faced a shaky future. It was located at the north end of the Strip, which was enjoying far less development than the south end, and it threatened to be forgotten as new, more exciting establishments opened down the street. The hotel's fate was finally sealed when Wynn imploded it to make room for his namesake.

Then he proceeded to seal this resort's future as well—this time for the good. When it opened in 2005, the Wynn Las Vegas housed 2,700 hotel rooms, 18 restaurants, 29 upscale stores, and even an on-site Ferrari and Maserati dealership. Guests could choose to entertain themselves either on the golf course with a 35-foot waterfall at the eighteenth hole; in the art gallery featuring Wynn's private collection, including Renoirs and Picassos; at the Broadway Theater, featuring the Tony Award–winning *Avenue* Q; or at the brand new show by Franco Dragone, creator of several Las Vegas Cirque du Soleil shows. All that cost about $2.7 billion—but an expansion was underway even before the resort opened. Harrah's chairman, Gary Loveman, who toured the resort before it opened, described it as "what God would build if He had the money."

Luxor Las Vegas

Not able to beat out the original Great Pyramids, which are among the eight wonders of the ancient world, the Luxor in Las Vegas just settled for the world's largest atrium, at 29 million cubic feet. With 30 stories, just over 4,400 rooms, and a 120,000-square-foot casino, the Luxor is also the second-largest hotel in the United States. The newest brainchild of Circus Circus executives opened on October 9, 1993, in strict adherence to the original concept of Jay Sarno, the company's builder: *always* stick to the theme. This time, that theme was Egyptian, hence venues at the Luxor include the Pharaoh's Pavilion, Nefertiti's Lounge, RA Nightclub, and the Nile Deli. The Pharaoh's Pavilion not only boasts an IMAX theater and arcade games, but also includes King Tut's Museum, which provides a self-guided tour of

ancient Egypt and its history and archaeology. In 2000, the Luxor broke the Las Vegas entertainment mold by importing Blue Man Group, three bald, blue men who have taken their multisensory show around the world and, since arriving on the Strip, have even shown up in computer commercials. As if all that didn't draw enough attention to the Mojave Desert's great pyramid, the world's brightest beam of light—visible even from Los Angeles when the sky is clear—has shot up from the Luxor's point miles into the darkness each and every night since the hotel opened. The beam signifies the Egyptian belief that the souls of those who climbed to the top of the pyramid would be transported straight to heaven. Those eager to test that theory should be aware that a 10-story sphinx stands guard at the Luxor, too.

The Venetian Resort Hotel Casino

Even before the Venetian's time, this spot on the Strip made a lot of history as the Sands hotel-casino. The legendary Sands opened in December 1952 with much to boast of: Entertainment was directed by Jack Entratter, who came to the Sands from the Copacabana, the legendary New York City night spot where he had known virtually every big-name entertainer in the country. The symbol of the Sands as the very heart of Strip entertainment was the so-called Rat Pack—Frank Sinatra, Dean Martin, Sammy Davis, Jr., Joey Bishop, and Peter Lawford—who played there as part of the "Summit at the Sands" in January 1960, during the filming of (the original) *Oceans 11* movie. All

but Lawford had been regulars in Las Vegas showrooms, especially at the Sands, but this event brought all of them together on stage. Each night during the summit, celebrities ranging from Bob Hope to Shirley MacLaine joined the famous five on stage. On one occasion they even introduced an audience member who happened to be running for president: Senator John F. Kennedy.

The Sands remained Sinatra's playground until Howard Hughes bought the establishment in 1967. That year was a bad one for Sinatra in general. First, his marriage to Mia Farrow was in trouble. Then along came Hughes, who revoked his unofficial license to do whatever he wanted at the Sands. Old Blue Eyes apparently was drunk the night he found out that he had run out of gambling credit. He went looking for casino manager Carl Cohen, who ended up socking him one. Sinatra then headed across the street to Caesars Palace, one of several Las Vegas venues in which he would go on to perform. He never returned to the Sands—wholly the Sands' loss.

In 1989, the Sands was purchased by Sheldon Adelson, the Massachusetts businessman who created the COMDEX computer trade show. Adelson eventually realized that the Sands could not compete with the Strip's new megaresorts, and so he imploded it on November 26, 1996. On May 3, 1999, Adelson's dream resort, the $1.5 billion Venetian, opened atop the Sands' dusty grave. The new complex includes a 500,000-square-foot indoor mall; reproductions of Venice's Grand Canal and St. Mark's Square; singing gondoliers who transport visitors through the property; the very first Madame Tussaud's museum in America; and a Guggenheim art museum. Adelson and his company recently added the Venezia Tower, and the next big enhancement is already underway: a $1.6 billion all-suite hotel called the Palazzo. Adelson hopes that the improved complex will be comparable to Rodeo Drive in Beverly Hills. With the "old" Venetian included, it will at least be a very fitting successor to Sinatra's old haunt.

Mandalay Bay Resort and Casino

Mandalay Bay is the newest—and poshest—addition to what has become known as the "miracle mile," a particularly fabulous mile of land once owned by the Mandalay Resort Group, which built the Excalibur and the Luxor along it, too. Opened in 1999, Mandalay Bay continued the Las Vegas theme trend with its tropical gardens, elephant statues, and Indian-sounding names for its shops and amenities. Mandalay diverged from this theme, however, in order to break different ground for the corporation that built it. For example, the resort's House of Blues features blues, jazz, and pop, and the popular vodka bar is called Red Square. (Red Square achieved cult status when the head disappeared from its massive statue of Lenin. It turned up at a thrift store and is now encased in ice inside the bar.) These features are hardly Indian in theme, but they are responsible for moving the Mandalay Bay into the world of first-class entertainment.

Mandalay Bay also enjoys unique distinction in Las Vegas as the site of the city's only Four Seasons Hotel. Their guests have their own separate check-in, restaurant, and pool and spa areas. In 2004, Mandalay added the businessman-oriented THEhotel, a $250 million, 1,118-room tower of suites with both bedroom and office—and no gambling. Then, to make the Mandalay complex even more attractive to business travelers, the hotel-casino proceeded to build a 1.4 million-square-foot convention center. The center reportedly was one of the factors that inspired MGM Mirage officials to seek a merger with the Mandalay Resort Group in 2005, a union of nearly $8 billion worth of luxurious hotels and great entertainment—just one more grand Las Vegas wedding.

Paris Las Vegas

Even though Las Vegas is better known for its Hispanic and Native American heritage, the city recently made room for a little French, too. On September 1, 1999, the $800 million Paris Las Vegas Hotel opened next to Bally's with 2,916 rooms on 34 floors. To say that the hotel-casino just has a French theme would be a terrible understatement: its nightclubs and lounges include Le Cabaret, Napoleon's, and Risqué; its restaurants include the Eiffel Tower Restaurant and Mon Ami Gabi; and its suites are the Suite LeMans and Suite Calais. As one might expect, the indoor shopping street is called Le Boulevard and includes a singing breadman and other employees in French costume.

The commercials advertising the hotel's impending opening warned of its intense French-ness by depicting various French landmarks being

The wedding chapel at Paris Las Vegas.

packed away to be moved to Las Vegas—and yes, there is actually a replica of the Eiffel Tower at Paris Las Vegas. Yet not everything at the Paris is French: the continuing entertainment in the showroom is *We Will Rock You*, the musical based on the story of the English group Queen, and there is a wider variety of food than just French cuisine. The Paris also made Las Vegas history when Robert Johnston, creator of Black Entertainment Television (BET), became the first African-American to hold a license for a business on the Strip, *Tres Jazz* at the Paris. Despite this occasional straying from the French theme, the Paris is still tres enjoyable.

The "dancing waters" in front of the Bellagio, rising and falling in rhythm with music.

Bellagio

Several Las Vegas hotel-casinos opened in 1955, and the sudden, intense competition and bad management drove a few out of business. At the corner of Flamingo and the Strip, the Dunes managed to survive its initial rough patch, thanks in part to its introduction of "Minsky's Follies," a burlesque show featuring topless women—the very first to be seen on the Las Vegas Strip. In the early 1980s, however, when a federal and state crackdown found its ties to organized-crime figures were a little closer than the law allowed, the Dunes could not be saved by lovely ladies.

Enter Steve Wynn. Wynn had raised the bar on the Strip with construction of the Mirage, and he raised it again by simply imploding the troubled Dunes in 1993 in order to build the Bellagio. The

Mediterranean-style resort modeled on Italy's Lake Como opened on October 15, 1998. The then-astronomical cost of $1.6 billion had bought it more than 3,000 state-of-the-art rooms and suites, as well as the Fountains of Bellagio, with more than 1,200 fountain jets that spray "dancing waters" over a distance of 1,000 feet and up to 460 feet above the 8.5-acre lake that hides the jets. The waters "dance" every half-hour to the blaring of opera and classical masterpieces, as well as to some pop and rock favorites.

Inside, the hotel's Conservatory and Botanical Gardens cover more than 13,000 square feet beneath a 50-foot-high glass ceiling, with rotating displays of flowers, plants, and trees. Via Bellagio, a long interior street, offers 100,000 square feet of high-end shopping and two restaurants with AAA five-star ratings—making the Bellagio the only hotel with two such distinguished restaurants. The Bellagio Gallery of Fine Art is home to many interesting permanent exhibits and hosts even more temporary ones. Another Cirque du Soleil show by writer-director Franco Dragone—called "O" because it sounds like the French word *eau*, which means water—plays in its own theater inside the Bellagio, combining acrobatics and music above, on, and in the indoor body of water.

Since MGM purchased the Bellagio from Wynn in 2000, it has continued to enhance the property: In 2004, it reopened the renovated Spa Bellagio and the new Spa Tower. Overhead walkways have connected the casinos at the corner of Flamingo and the Strip for some time now, but the Bellagio added a tram to the Monte Carlo in 2005. As if anybody would ever want to leave the Bellagio!

The Palms Casino Hotel

Unlike most well-known Las Vegas resorts, the Palms is privately owned. Its mastermind is George Maloof, who sought to attract a youthful clientele to the resort—beautiful people with money to spend. But the establishment leads a bit of a double-life. Las Vegas journalist Geoff Schumacher may have described it best when he called it a "locals-friendly casino by day, youth-oriented hotspot by night." At its opening in 2001, the $268 million hotel included 455 rooms in a tower topped off by the 55th-floor Ghostbar lounge. The 25,000-square-foot, three-level Rain in the Desert nightclub featured a waterfall that could be turned into a screen. The Palms benefited from several publicity coups: not only did quite a few young celebrities make it their hangout, but the hotel-casino was the site of a season-long taping of MTV's *The Real World* reality show, and it hosted several film festivals, *Playboy* magazine's fiftieth anniversary celebration, and not least of all, pop singer Britney Spears' first wedding (which was later annulled).

Luckily, the Palms has had better luck than Spears. In 2004, Maloof announced that he would build a 40-story, 347-room tower with 46 suites and sky penthouses, plus an 8,000-square-foot recording studio. In March 2005 came plans for Palms Place: a 599-unit hotel/condominium tower with a private, gated entry and 50,000-square-foot pool, with condos ranging from 600 to 7,000 square feet and costing from $500,000 to $7 million.

Rio All-Suite Casino Hotel

The Rio opened in 1990 as something truly different: an all-suite hotel with less than 500 rooms in an unusual red and blue decor, built at a cost of just $85 million. Its history has also been different from other successful hotels that opened small and grew with time. The Rio's builder was MarCor, a sister operation of the construction company Marnell Corrao Associates that had developed retail and office complexes. The owners hoped to attract business over from the Gold Coast, a more locals-oriented hotel-casino next door. They turned increasingly to a Caribbean theme, engaged in several major hotel and casino expansions, and began targeting a younger crowd.

This plan worked so well that Harrah's bought the Rio in 1998 for $888 million. While the Rio was relatively new, Harrah's had long been part of the Nevada fabric. William Harrah came to Reno and opened a bingo club in the 1940s. He gradually expanded, building new hotel-casinos that put a premium on entertainment. His company eventually moved into Las Vegas by purchasing the Holiday Casino on the Strip, which it turned into Harrah's. In the 1990s, Harrah acquired the Showboat Corporation, not so much for the old hotel on Boulder Highway as for the Showboat's lucrative operations in Atlantic City and Sydney, Australia. About the same time, Harrah's purchase of the Rio gave the company entrée to a younger customer base. Particularly appealing to this younger crowd are the Rio's popular buffet and other varied dining choices, entertainment like the Voodoo Lounge and shows featuring Penn & Teller, Chippendales, and a more recent addition called Erocktica.

Other Sides of the Strip: Fun Without Gambling!

Previous page: The Liberace Museum is just one part of an entire plaza dedicated largely to "Mr. Showmanship."

"Welcome to Fabulous Las Vegas Nevada" Sign

Since 1959, the "Welcome to Fabulous Las Vegas Nevada" sign has been every Las Vegas visitor's first welcome onto the Strip. It is probably the most famous, readily recognizable symbol of Las Vegas throughout the world. It is located well past Mandalay Bay on Las Vegas Boulevard South, which most people would consider the beginning of the south end of the Strip. However, Las Vegas Boulevard was also once Highway 91, the road built in the 1920s to carry drivers from Los Angeles to Salt Lake City. When *those* drivers came through town in the 1960s and '70s, it was the "Welcome to Las Vegas" sign that let them know they had arrived in Sin City.

Clark County bought the sign for $4,000 from its designer, Betty Willis. Willis got her start in the 1940s as a commercial artist, and began designing neon signs in the 1950s. This sign features a flickering, two-toned, eight-point star and seven silver dollars, one for each of the letters in "Welcome." The sign is particularly suited to the city: after all, the stars certainly come out in Las Vegas, and the silver dollars bring to mind not only the gambling that awaits the welcomed, but also a bit of Nevada's history as the Silver State.

In the early 1970s, county officials discussed tearing down the sign, but local residents objected. The sign was used on an endless array of memorabilia when the city celebrated its centennial in 2005, making it today not just a symbol of the twinkling little desert star of the 1950s, but of the bright and shining constellation that is Las Vegas in the 21st century.

Showcase Mall

The Strip has more than just great entertainers—it *is* great entertainment itself, and the Showcase Mall is the classic example. It opened in July 1997, the brainchild of businessmen Barry Fieldman and Bob Unger. They liked the vertical retail center concept used at such centers as the Warner Bros. Studio Store in Manhattan and Sony in Chicago, and they decided to try it in Las Vegas on a small plot of land they controlled near the MGM Grand.

Those who venture inside get to relive their memories as a kid in a candy store—literally. M&M/Mars and Ethel M Chocolates opened a retail center there, and various restaurants offer "real food." But the Showcase Mall has plenty even for those who don't come to eat and drink. Dieting and already-full visitors rediscover their inner child at the very first movie theaters on the Strip; the GameWorks arcade, created by Steven Spielberg, DreamWorks SKG, Sega, and Universal Studios, with games based on the movies *Jurassic Park*, *Star Wars*, and *Twister*; the Grand Canyon Experience; and the Houdini Magic Shop—to name just a few.

Not everything has worked out so well at the Showcase Mall. The Las Vegas World of Coca Cola branch, modeled after the original in Atlanta, closed in 2000, and so did the All-Star Café, owned by several major sports athletes, including Tiger Woods, Shaquille O'Neal, Wayne Gretzky, Monica Seles, Ken Griffey, Jr., and Las Vegan Andre Agassi. But all in all, the fun still continues, and new ideas are being realized every day. Most recently, in February 2005, the San Francisco-based company City Center Retail and its New York partner, Angelo Gordon, bought the complex and began making plans to add more retail space and even condominiums.

The world's largest Coke bottle beckons both kids and adults into the world's largest playground, the Showcase Mall.

Elvis-A-Rama Museum

After Presley's well-visited Graceland mansion in Memphis, Las Vegas is probably the place most closely associated with the beloved pop culture icon. Presley signed with RCA Records in 1954, and in 1956 was booked at the New Frontier. The show was a failure—at least Presley's part of it—due to an awkward mix of personalities. Freddy Martin, an orchestra leader; Martin's singer and piano player, Merv Griffin; and Shecky Greene, widely considered the greatest comedian ever to set foot in Las Vegas—these were the veteran stars with whom the 21-year-old budding teenage heartthrob had to compete for audience attention.

But Presley was far from finished with Las Vegas. In 1963, he returned to film *Viva Las Vegas* with Ann-Margret, who went on to her own successful career as a Vegas headliner. In 1967, Presley married his longtime girlfriend, Priscilla Beaulieu, at the Aladdin Hotel. And in 1969, he made his famous comeback at the International. His manager promptly signed a five-year contract for him at the hotel for $125,000 a week for four weeks a year. That meant a $2 million expense for the International over the life of Presley's contract, but he brought in enormous showroom business for the hotel—and his manager would lose a lot more at the gambling tables there, anyway.

Elvis remained a Las Vegas superstar until his death in 1977, and today the city still pays him tribute on Industrial Road, just west of the Strip. Owned by Chris Davidson, who started his collecting career with the simple purchase of two of Presley's checks and a personal letter, the Elvis-A-Rama Museum is now the world's largest private collection of Elvis Presley memorabilia. The museum boasts more than 2,000 items, including three of the King's cars, his stage clothes, clothes from his films, and an assortment of documents and letters—plus live shows by Elvis impersonators. As the Elvis-A-Rama Museum shows, in death as in life, the King of Rock 'n Roll is *still* King of Las Vegas.

The Little Church of the West

Las Vegas has hundreds of chapels and churches to marry in, but the Little Church of the West is special. It opened at the Hotel Last Frontier in 1942, and for many years it was known as "the hitching post." Indeed, *many* have gotten hitched there: Pin-up idol Betty Grable and bandleader Harry James, who lived in Las Vegas and frequently performed at Strip hotel-casinos, were the first celebrities to do so. Though Elvis Presley married Priscilla at the Aladdin, he wed Ann-Margret at Little Church of the West—and this is where the wedding scene was shot for the movie *Viva Las Vegas*—so the site is popular with Elvis fans. Considering how many weddings Mickey Rooney and Zsa Zsa Gabor have each had, it was inevitable that they would stop off there at least once, too. Then followed Richard Gere and Cindy Crawford, Fernando Lamas and Arlene Dahl, Judy Garland and Mark Herron, and so many more.

The church is actually considered historic enough to appear on the National Register of Historic Places. It's also one of those rare Las Vegas buildings that has been moved several times: When the Hotel Last Frontier gave way to the New Frontier, the Little Church of the West building was moved slightly north to another side of the hotel, then shifted to the south edge of the Hacienda property (now Mandalay Bay) in 1978. It moved again in 1996, this time to its present location at the far southern end of the Strip, by the Russell Road exit from Interstate 15. Las Vegans say that, like marriage itself, the Little Church of the West adapts to circumstances.

Fashion Show

That Howard Hughes significantly affected Las Vegas is a well-known fact, but his influence survives today in some ways that people don't expect. Since his heirs sold all his hotel properties, most of them have been replaced. But the Fashion Show mall in the middle of the Strip—standing right between the Frontier, which was once owned by Hughes, and the Mirage, which was built where Hughes' Castaways hotel-casino used to stand—still recalls him loud and clear.

Fashion Show is one of the few Las Vegas establishments that manages to serve both of the city's two very different markets: locals and tourists. Since its 1981 opening, this popularity has forced it to double its original 822,700 square feet of retail space. In 1996, the Rouse Co. acquired the Howard Hughes Corporation and teamed with the mall's tenants on a $1 billion, 900,000-square-foot expansion, including a 128-foot-tall structure called "The Cloud" that hovers over the mall like... well, a cloud. Then, in late 2004, Chicago-based General Growth Properties acquired Rouse—and with it the Fashion Show—for $12.6 billion. The mall now houses 250 high-end shops and retailers, as well as numerous up-scale restaurants.

The Liberace Museum

In a city of outstanding entertainers and spectacles, no one has stood out more than Liberace. For a man nicknamed "Mr. Showmanship," there could be no more appropriate place than Las Vegas. The piano prodigy played nightclubs, made films, starred in his own television program, recorded albums, and sold out concerts around the world—but he was always most closely associated with the Strip.

Liberace made his Las Vegas debut in November 1944 at the Hotel Last Frontier. One day at rehearsal, he found a man standing by the light board and, thinking that he was the lighting technician, started explaining to him how the lights worked. Entertainment director Maxine Lewis approached the two and said to Liberace with an air of surprise, "I didn't realize you knew Howard Hughes." Later, as the performer who opened the brand new Riviera in 1955, Liberace earned a then-mind-boggling salary of $50,000 a week. He continued to star regularly in Strip showrooms until just before his death in 1987.

In 1979, Liberace opened the Liberace Museum to display his fabulous possessions, arranged to trace the development of his life and career. The museum's first building spotlights his piano and automobile collections. The second features his costumes, jewelry, and home decorations—some of which are displayed in a rotating gallery—including the famous red-white-and-blue-sequined hot pants he wore in Australia, the world's largest rhinestone, and one of the world's only two hand-made Moser crystal service sets from Czechoslovakia (the other belongs to Queen Elizabeth II).

The museum not only preserves an important part of Las Vegas history—which Liberace certainly was—it is the perfect embodiment of the personality of the showman known for his penchant to say during shows, "Pardon me while I slip into something more spectacular."

Turquoise Mandarin cape worn by Liberace during his tours in 1983.

Liberace's 9-foot, mirrored rhinestone Baldwin concert grand piano, which he played in his 1986 farewell appearance at Radio City Music Hall.

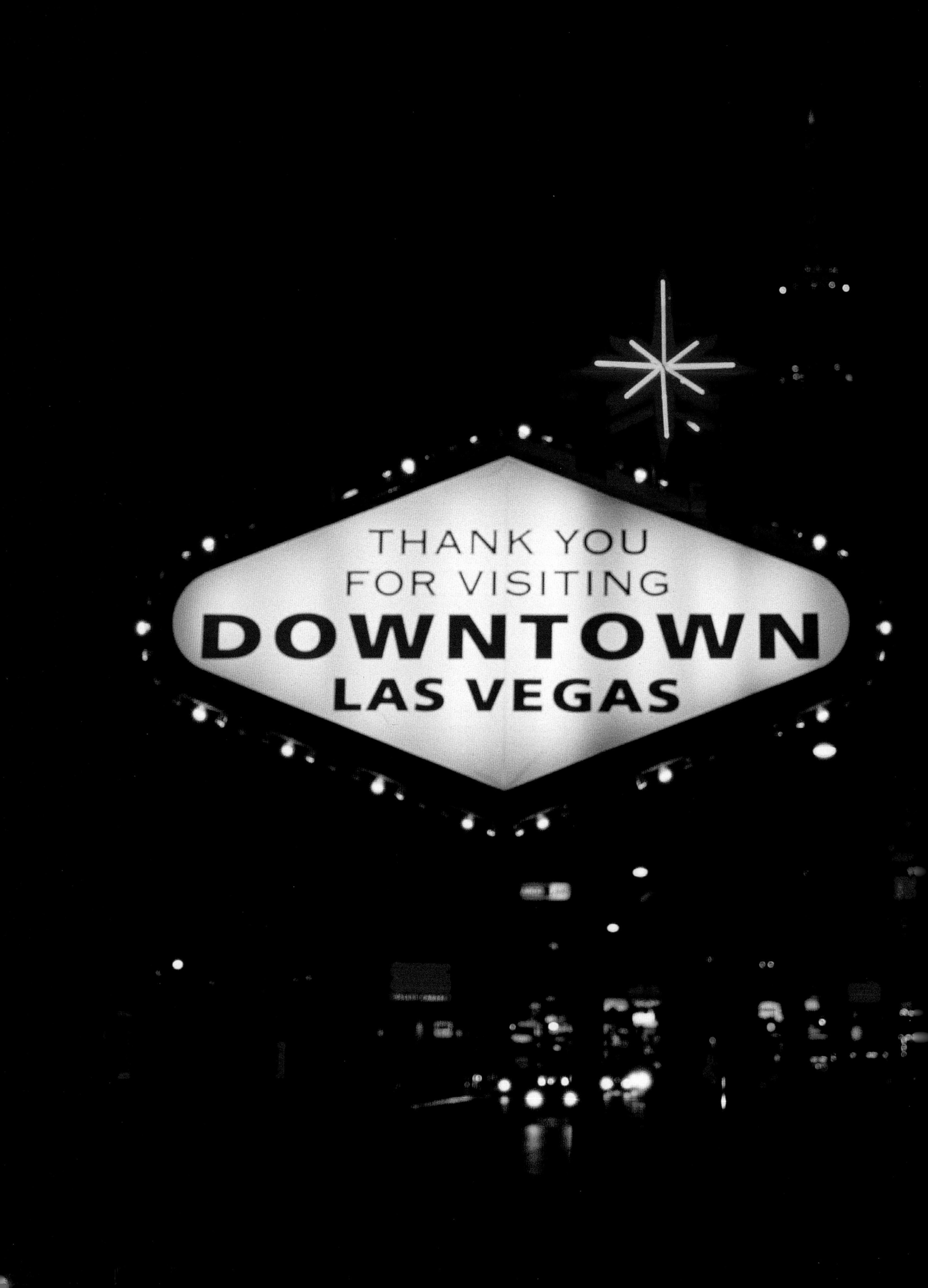
THANK YOU
FOR VISITING
DOWNTOWN
LAS VEGAS

Downtown and Beyond: More Gambling, Different Neighborhood

Binion's Gambling Hall & Hotel

If the Horseshoe can be called a Las Vegas legend, it's only because Benny Binion and his family are so legendary themselves. The hotel-casino occupies the 1932 building that originally housed Las Vegas' first air-conditioned hotel, and Binion opened the Horseshoe on the ground floor in 1951.

Binion had run illegal casinos in Dallas, where he had a reputation for being tough. He must have been, because he allegedly tried to kill his Dallas rival Herbert Noble several times, and Noble was once caught boarding his private plane in Texas carrying two bombs and a map of Las Vegas—with an X marking Binion's house.

At the Horseshoe, Binion introduced several innovations to the downtown casino industry: He raised the limits on table games. Limousines were sent to the airport to pick up guests. And the Horseshoe was the first downtown casino to replace the usual sawdust with carpeting. That was all part of Binion's strategy to "make little people feel like big people."

In 1953, Binion went to jail for income tax evasion, and thereafter he could never be licensed again. Still, he clearly continued to run the operation, and it was a tremendous success. When asked how he did it, Binion explained: "Good food cheap, good whiskey cheap, and a good gamble. That's all there is to it, son."

When Benny Binion died in 1989, his children, Becky, Jack, and Ted, continued to run the Horseshoe. Then the already-famous family started getting really notorious: In 1996, Becky had a falling-out with Jack that wound up in court. Becky ended up with the Horseshoe; Jack owned the family's other properties. Ted died in 1998, and a jury convicted his girlfriend and her lover of his murder; the Nevada Supreme Court overturned the results on appeal and a subsequent trial led to a not-guilty verdict. Becky proved unable to manage a casino and wound up selling the Horseshoe. The out-of-state company now in control of the property renamed it Binion's Gambling Hall & Hotel— evidence, perhaps, of the fame and power of the Binion name, inside and outside Las Vegas.

Pages 108–109: Welcome to Downtown Las Vegas sign.

El Cortez Hotel & Casino

The history of El Cortez' ownership is like a line-up of famous—and infamous—Las Vegas personalities. Marion Hicks, the mastermind who originally built the establishment, was one of several entrepreneurs who moved to Las Vegas in the late 1930s and early 1940s. He had operated a gambling boat off of Long Beach, California until state authorities shut it down. At the same time, the same authorities closed casinos belonging to Tony Cornero (who had built the Meadows in Las Vegas) and Wilbur Clark (who later founded the Desert Inn), both of whom also moved to Las Vegas as a result. To help him obtain funding and licenses for the construction of El Cortez, Hicks turned for help

to a Las Vegan, a young attorney named Cliff Jones, who would later become the lieutenant governor. In November 1941, Hicks opened El Cortez for $245,000—a rather impressive sum for a Las Vegas casino in those days.

Since then, some of the biggest names in Las Vegas history have operated El Cortez. Details about the venture are murky, but Bugsy Siegel once bought the hotel-casino with his old friend Moe Sedway and recent Las Vegas arrivals Davie Berman and Willie Alderman—all old allies of Meyer Lansky, the financial brains behind much of American organized crime from the 1930s to the 1970s. They wound up selling the property after fighting apparently broke out within the

group, and Siegel plowed the profits into building the Flamingo.

The new owners were experienced Las Vegas gaming operators with far better reputations. Kell Houssels had opened the Las Vegas Club in 1930 and went on to run the Showboat, the Tropicana, and other local businesses. Bill Moore had built the Hotel Last Frontier with his uncle, R. E. Griffith. In 1963, Houssels and Moore sold El Cortez to Jackie Gaughan, who had first visited El Cortez while on leave from the Army Air Corps in 1943. Gaughan had gotten his start in bookmaking in 1936, while still a teenager in Nebraska. There he met Ed Barrick, a legendary bookmaker who taught Gaughan a great deal about the casino business, and with whom he invested in the Flamingo and other casinos.

Barrick eventually married, and his wife Marjorie became a leading local philanthropist, endowing a UNLV lecture series and giving her name to the school's natural history museum.

Gaughan went on to build a whole network of profitable locals' casinos. At one point, he owned all or part of Union Plaza, Showboat, Western,

Gold Spike, Las Vegas Club, and Nevada Club. His son Michael followed in his footsteps with the Coast Casinos, including the Barbary Coast, Gold Coast, Suncoast, and Orleans, and most recently the South Coast south of the Strip, which is still under construction.

Jackie Gaughan sold Union Plaza, the Las Vegas Club, Gold Spike, and the Western to Barrick Gaming—oddly, no relation to his old partner—but he kept El Cortez and still maintains a residence there. He continues the establishment's tradition of paycheck giveaways, in which customers who cash their paychecks at the casino spin a wheel to see if they can double their money or win prizes. He also introduced a brand new invention that since has spread like wildfire around Las Vegas: the "fun book," a simple book of coupons for local restaurants and entertainment. Together, Gaughan and his son Michael are one of Las Vegas' greatest success stories. As Michael explained: "My Dad and I have an agreement. He tries to get everything north of Sahara Avenue and I try to get everything south of it."

Fremont Hotel and Casino

The Fremont Hotel was named for the street it's on, but the street's namesake is John C. Frémont, the nineteenth-century military officer and explorer who literally put Las Vegas on the map that he drew in a federal report on his Western travels. The Fremont Hotel is famous in its own right, too, though: the 15-story hotel opened in 1956 as the first high-rise in downtown Las Vegas. It was also the first to offer big-name entertainment and fine restaurants downtown, plus it hosted a television station that broadcast from inside the property, thereby adding to the excitement of visiting the establishment.

Though onlookers assumed that everything at the Fremont was going well, it actually kept running into some pretty serious trouble. First, Eddie Levinson, one of the Fremont's main investors, got embroiled in a scandal involving Bobby Baker, a close friend of Lyndon Johnson. Then one of the hotel's later owners, Allen Glick

and his Argent Corporation, turned out to be fronts for Midwestern organized-crime syndicates. The state forced Glick's departure, but the money-skimming continued under the new ownership. Finally, the owners' licenses were revoked in 1983, and the state asked Boyd Gaming to take over. They agreed to run the Fremont for the state, and later they bought the property for themselves.

Befitting the Boyd family's long ties to the Hawaiian market, they changed the Fremont's look and feel to emphasize Polynesian and tropical dining and themes. The Fremont now calls itself the heartbeat of downtown Las Vegas. Indeed, something like arteries now connects it to other Boyd properties nearby: a bridge runs from the Fremont to the California Hotel, with stores and dining between the two, and another bridge leads from the California to Main Street Station.

Golden Nugget Hotel

The Golden Nugget was erected in 1946, but it enjoys the distinction of sitting on the original Las Vegas townsite, which the railroad auctioned off in 1905. The hotel-casino's builders were members of a local group led by Guy McAfee that came together just for the project. In the early 1970s, Mel Wolzinger, Earl Wilson, and Steve Wynn purchased the relatively modest downtown property with the intent of creating there a downtown resort experience that would rival the Strip getaways. Wynn persuaded city officials to close down Carson Street to allow him to expand. There he added a coffee shop and a tower to the original property. Next he expanded the Golden Nugget name into Atlantic City and signed Frank Sinatra to an exclusive contract that

made Old Blue Eyes the headliner at all his properties and the star of television commercials advertising them. (In one, Wynn introduces himself, but Sinatra doesn't recognize the name and asks, confused, "Who?" Finding out that Wynn is the owner of the resort, Sinatra asks for towels.)

Wynn soon enjoyed the honor of having turned the Golden Nugget into downtown's largest resort, with more than 1,900 rooms, several restaurants, and lots of big-name entertainment. In 2000, however, he sold the property to MGM, who later sold to Tim Poster and Tom Breitling, the young dot.com millionaires who founded Travel-scape (now Expedia). In early 2005, they announced the Golden Nugget's sale to Landry's Restaurants. Ownership may change, but the Golden Nugget remains a key part of downtown.

SAM'S TOWN
HOTEL & GAMBLING HALL
WELCOME
LARGE TRUCKS & BUSES
DO NOT ENTER
CLEARANCE
9'-0"

Sam's Town Hotel & Gambling Hall

The "Sam" in "Sam's Town" refers to Sam Boyd, who came to Las Vegas in the early 1940s after working as a dealer in southern California and Hawaii. He started out his career as a dealer and worked his way up the casino ladder, eventually becoming executive and part-owner at the Mint, a downtown hotel where he designed promotions to appeal to local customers. In 1971, Boyd and partners Jackie Gaughan, J. Kell Houssels, Jr., and Frank Scott built the Union Plaza, where Boyd introduced what was then a somewhat controversial innovation: women casino dealers. Boyd sold his interest there within a couple of years and built the California Hotel and Casino, then began looking beyond downtown.

In 1979, Sam Boyd and his son, Bill, opened Sam's Town Hotel and Gambling Hall on Boulder Highway, the road that leads to Hoover Dam and on to Arizona. There they pursued a Western theme that was epitomized by the Sam's Town Western Emporium and catered to locals with cheap food, entertainment, and bowling. The latter, rather unusual feature was a deliberate challenge to the Showboat, which had opened a quarter of a century before and boasted 106 bowling lanes and a nationally televised annual Professional Bowlers' Tour event.

Sam's Town has grown since then, adding more rooms, an RV park, movie theaters, restaurants, a 1,100-seat event center, and the Mystic Falls Indoor Park, complete with restaurants and, of course, a waterfall. In addition to bowlers, Sam's Town now attracts the NASCAR crowd by sponsoring Busch Series Grand National Division Races and the Sam's Town 300 at the Las Vegas Motor Speedway northeast of town. Boyd Gaming itself has also expanded, and now includes not only Sam's Town, but also the Stardust on the Strip, several downtown properties, Michael Gaughan's Coast Casinos, and the Borgata in Atlantic City, which it runs in partnership with MGM Mirage.

The horse and cowboy sign from the now-closed Hacienda Hotel ride on as part of a downtown neon exhibit at the Fremont Street Experience.

Opposite: The world's largest big-screen television—spanning the width of five football fields—beneath the 3-block canopy that is the Fremont Street Experience.

Fremont Street looks a bit different today than it did when the Las Vegas townsite was born on May 15, 1905. Back then, Fremont was dusty: the railroad that controlled the town took 20 years to pave all five blocks of it from Main Street to Fifth Street (now Las Vegas Boulevard). Beginning at the Union Pacific Railroad depot, Fremont represented the town's main drag, and it was quickly filled, first with wooden, then brick buildings. From Main to Third, most of those buildings housed stores and hotels, and smaller businesses and residences occupied the houses from Third up to Fifth.

Once wide-open gambling began in the 1930s, the once-humble Fremont Street became known as Glitter Gulch. Most of the early Las Vegas casinos operated on the block, mixed with other businesses. It remained the town's main drag, but as the Strip grew in the 1940s and 1950s, Fremont Street began to lose ground in the battle for tourist dollars. Its problems worsened in the 1980s, when neighborhood casinos such as the Stations Casinos began to draw away some of Fremont Street's local business. Las Vegas then faced a problem most cities experience sooner or later: what to do when the urban core begins to decline.

Local business and government officials tossed around a variety of ideas, including Las Venice, which would have brought canals and boats to the sandy streets. Instead, they settled on the $70 million Fremont Street Experience, an idea presented by noted urban designer Jon Jerde. The "experience" debuted in 1995: the world's largest big screen, spanning the length of five football fields and supported by 16 columns weighing 26,000 pounds each, all sheltered beneath a canopy that covers three whole blocks of Fremont Street. Every evening, a show is presented every hour, on the hour, with 550,000 watts of crystal-clear sound blasted through the high-tech sound system, and 12.5 million LED modules transmitting a perfect, high-resolution picture—an astounding phenomenon the city

named Viva Vision. The ten casinos and 60 restaurants that line the block agreed to dim their neon during the shows, but they probably don't lose any business because of it: most visitors only stop to ooh and aah before heading in to gamble or dine.

In addition to the opportunity to just walk and gawk, free public concerts by a variety of artists are a regular part of the Fremont Street Experience. Just east of the canopy is Neonopolis, a $100 million retail center with a 14-screen movie complex. As Las Vegas celebrated its centennial, passers-by had even more to gawk at along Fremont Street: an outdoor, neon museum of classic Las Vegas signs, formerly the occupants of a "boneyard" a few blocks from downtown, but cleaned up and brought back to life just in time for the celebration.

Stratosphere Las Vegas

Every community has its maverick. For Las Vegas, the most important maverick in recent years has been Bob Stupak—and the reason why is easy to see. Born and raised in Pittsburgh as the son of a gambling operator, Stupak started out selling two-for-one coupon books, then moved to Australia, where he ran a successful telemarketing business. He introduced himself to Las Vegas by opening Bob Stupak's World Famous Historic Gambling Museum. When that burned down, he opened Vegas World in 1979 with a 20-story tower, a gaudy exterior, high-limit games, coupon books (of course), and the motto "The Sky's the Limit."

When a windstorm blew down the Vegas World sign, Stupak thought the winds were telling him to take his motto more seriously. Instead of putting the sign back up, he planned the Stratosphere Tower, based on the Seattle

The Stratosphere Tower, reaching more than 1,000 feet into the sky.

Space Needle and the Sydney Tower in Australia. His only problem was financing the elaborate idea, but Stupak solved that problem (for a while) by taking in a partner: Lyle Berman, of Grand Casinos in Minnesota. The Stratosphere opened in April 1996 at a cost of $550 million. The top of the 1,149-foot tower featured a restaurant, the "Big Shot" ride, which shoots riders toward the sky, and a roller coaster with 840 feet of track suspended 909 feet above the ground.

Many came to see the Stratosphere Tower, but few stayed in the hotel or gambled in the casino. Stupak and Berman had a falling-out, and eventually billionaire financier Carl Icahn took over the entire establishment, made renovations, and improved the bottom line. Stupak occasionally makes noises about re-entering the gaming industry, but the Stratosphere will most likely be his greatest achievement—and that is certainly nothing to be ashamed of.

Moulin Rouge

Although it closed within just a few months, the Moulin Rouge played a significant role in Las Vegas history. At the time of its opening on May 24, 1955, African-American entertainers could perform in the showrooms of Strip casinos, but were otherwise barred from the properties. The Moulin Rouge, advertised as interracial from the very beginning, gave them a place to both play *and* stay. The establishment earned a reputation as a hangout for black entertainers, and other—white—entertainers would join them there. In addition, even though the casino's ownership was mostly white, it provided jobs and opportunities for Las Vegas' long-segregated African-American community.

The establishment's untimely closing stemmed from a variety of financial problems (that were totally unrelated to its race policy). Before its lights went out, however, the Moulin Rouge became the scene of a couple of major moments in Las Vegas civil rights history. In 1960, Las Vegas NAACP president James McMillan, the city's first African-American dentist, threatened a national boycott and a march if the Strip and downtown properties continued to ban black customers. When the casino operators agreed to admit blacks, they met with McMillan and several civil rights leaders—black and white—at the Rouge to finalize the new policy. Also, the hotel-casino's longest-tenured owner, Sarann Knight-Preddy, was the first African-American woman to hold a Nevada gaming license.

Sadly, after its addition to the National Register of Historic Places, the Moulin Rouge burned down May 29, 2003. The hotel-casino's original sign and a little bit of the complex survived the fire and can still be seen, and city tours that specialize in African-American history and entertainment often visit the site.

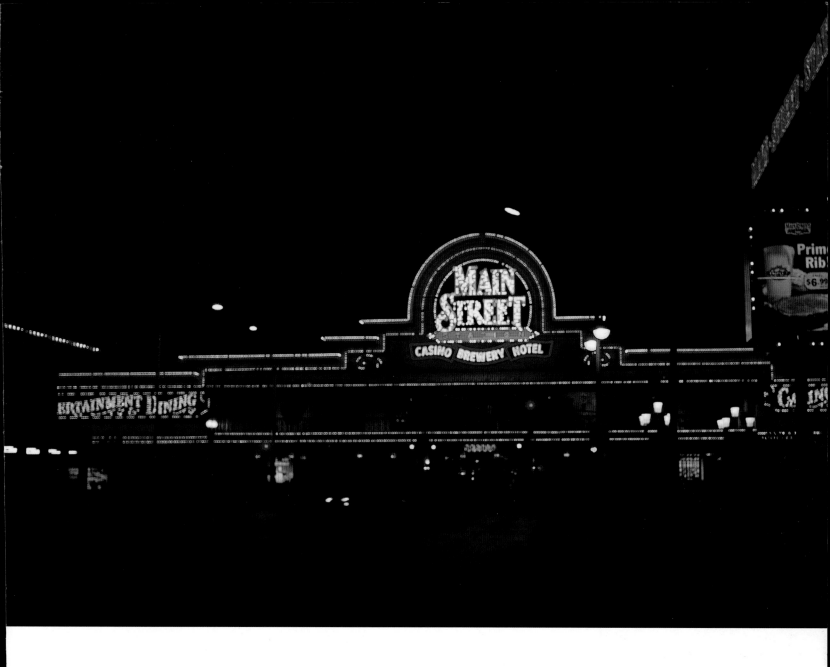

Main Street Station Hotel and Casino

In the late 1980s, the city went looking for someone to help with its downtown redevelopment efforts, and they found Bob Snow, owner of the successful Church Street Station in Orlando. With $17 million in taxpayer money from the city, Snow bought the Main Street Park Hotel and began transforming it.

The immediate results were all that Las Vegas officials could have hoped for . . . but the end result couldn't have been worse. The $82 million Main Street Station opened on August 30, 1991 with a Victorian theme that featured expensive antiques and beautiful hardwood floors and paneling. From that happy day on, the venture was a disaster: it was badly designed, it was off the beaten path, the old hotel's rooms were a stark—and disappointing—contrast to the new casino. To top it off, Snow, a hotelman, was trying to operate the casino himself without much knowledge about the business. At year's end, Snow filed for bankruptcy, and the property closed in June 1992.

A year later, Boyd Gaming came to the rescue. It turned the Triple 7 Brewpub into a popular downtown hangout and built a bridge that connected Main Street Station to its California Hotel, making casino-hopping easier and more enjoyable for guests and simultaneously streamlining their establishments' internal operations. Main Street Station is now a brilliant success, and city officials are happy again.

Guggenheim Hermitage MUSEUM

the Pursuit of Pleasure

Boccioni
Degas
Hals
Manet
Picasso
Rodin
Rubens
Titian

Guggenheim Hermitage MUSEUM

the Pursuit of Pleasure

Boccioni
Degas
Hals
Manet
Picasso
Rodin
Rubens
Titian

Guggenheim Hermitage MUSEUM

The Real Las Vegas: (Mostly) Normal Places to Live and Go

Previous page: The Guggenheim Hermitage Museum, at the Venetian resort hotel casino.

Above: View of Summerlin from one of its golf courses, Bear's Best Golf Club, personally designed by Jack Nicklaus.

Summerlin

Named for Howard Hughes' grandmother, Jean Amelia Summerlin, this beautiful master-planned community has simultaneously everything and nothing to do with Hughes himself. In the 1950s, he obtained 25,000 acres northwest of Las Vegas. He planned to move his aircraft company there from southern California, but his scientists refused to move to the desert, so he scrapped that idea. From that time on, Hughes never concerned himself personally with the site again.

Husite, as the site became known (look for it: HUghes' SITE), sat vacant for decades. In the early 1980s, the people at Howard Hughes Corporation (HHC) began making plans to turn the lot into a residential community. The first elements to be built in the neighborhood were the Meadows School, the first Del Webb Sun City community in Las Vegas, and finally Summerlin Parkway. When those were completed, HHC hired the man who had developed Green Valley for the Greenspun family, Mark Fine, to take charge in Summerlin.

The 1990s brought amazing growth to Las Vegas in general, and to its northwest portion in particular, and Summerlin was at the heart of it all. Fine set to work on a series of 300- to 1,000-acre villages, each with its own schools, parks, churches, and other community facilities—including several golf courses. By 1992, just one year after development began, Summerlin was already the nation's top-rated community in new home sales. To this day, Summerlin is still building, and its popularity seems unlikely to flag anytime soon.

Lake Las Vegas

Surrounding the 320-acre manmade Lake Las Vegas is a nearly 3,600-acre, master-planned development that has become one of the nation's most renowned upscale residential communities. To many locals, Lake Las Vegas symbolizes the growth and maturation of southern Nevada, just as Hoover Dam and Lake Mead made possible much of the growth of Las Vegas itself.

The original idea for the Lake Las Vegas community came from businessman J. Carlton Adair, who went bankrupt in the early 1970s after more than a decade of working on the project. Others tried to obtain financing and approval, but the plan always seemed either a too-distant dream or just plain dead. Then, in 1988, Transcontinental Properties bought out the most recent developer. Unlike the others, they followed through and, in 1990, named the area Lake Las Vegas. They built a dam to create the neighborhood's namesake lake, then started building homes and the development's special amenity: the South Shore Golf Club, designed by legendary golfer Jack Nicklaus, who since has designed another Lake Las Vegas course, Reflection Bay.

Today, Lake Las Vegas includes several communities and a host of amenities. Multi-million dollar homes dot the landscape, one of which belongs to Celine Dion, who moved there when she started performing regularly in her own show at Caesars Palace.

The Lakes

Numerous hotels and communities boast of their man-made bodies of water, but the Lakes is the residential development that really began it all. Located southwest of town, the 1,300-acre neighborhood is another brainchild of Al and Martin Collins, who have developed numerous residential projects in Las Vegas over the last half-century. The Collins brothers began planning the Lakes in the early 1980s, and the community has since become extremely popular for its highly esthetic and practical organization: the homes radiate out from the manmade lake, which is surrounded by stores and shops.

The Collins' development received much of its early attention as a result of a bank controversy—that thankfully proved to be a net gain for all. In 1984, Citicorp decided to build a credit-card processing plant at the Lakes, but Nevada law at the time did not allow out-of-state banks to open branches in Nevada. But local political and business leaders recognized that all of those credit-card bills marked with a Las Vegas return address would be good publicity for the area. State legislators soon changed the law, and Citicorp moved in. It turned out, however, that Citicorp chose to use the Lakes as its return address, reasoning that the city of Las Vegas still had a questionable reputation and cardholders might be concerned about receiving a bill from the gambling capital of the world. There was some public outcry, but the controversy soon died down, and the Lakes has been flourishing ever since.

Las Vegas Chinatown Plaza

Chinatowns have been part of American cityscapes for well over a century. Usually they have resulted from discrimination and segregation of Chinese immigrants by the white majority, but sometimes these immigrants have simply wanted to live together in familiar surroundings and to preserve their culture. The history of Las Vegas' Chinatown is distinctly different from both of these trends, however. The city never has had a large Chinese population, and so it was necessary for entrepreneurs to create a Chinatown of their own initiative. That's no surprise in Las Vegas, the city in which Venetian canals flow and Hawaiian volcanoes erupt right beside the Eiffel Tower and an ancient pyramid. It is unusual in the United States, though, which had never known an engineered Chinatown until Las Vegas made one.

Perhaps because there were already several Asian restaurants and stores a couple miles west of the Strip, on Spring Mountain Road between Valley View and Decatur, developer James Chih-Cheng Chen built an Asian mall there in 1995. Over the next three years, he added an imperial arch at the entry, a golden statue in the parking

A statue depicting characters from of the famous Chinese folk story "Xi You Ji (Journey to the West)" stands in Chinatown Plaza.

lot, and a two-tiered shopping center. Now called Las Vegas Chinatown Plaza, the complex is home to a variety of Asian supermarkets and Nevada's only Chinese bookstore. As the city's unofficial host of Chinese New Year celebrations and other cultural events, the plaza has become an anchor of the Las Vegas Asian community. With nine delicious, authentic restaurants, it's quickly becoming a popular attraction for locals and tourists out for good food, too.

Green Valley

Green Valley is the community that started the modern trend toward master-planned communities in southern Nevada. The first chapter of its story begins during World War II, when the Basic Magnesium plant that created the industrial town of Henderson was built. The second chapter was written by Hank Greenspun, a war veteran and New York lawyer who chose Las Vegas as his home. Soon he owned a news-paper, a golf course, the first local television station, and more than 3,500 acres of land in the Henderson area.

Greenspun lacked the money to develop his land, though, and so he turned much of the managerial responsibility for it over to his then-son-in-law, Mark Fine. Fine sold some of the land to fund development of the rest, then started building. By the late 1980s, the opening of

Green Valley Ranch, the latest addition to one of southern Nevada's most popular places to live.

The District at Green Valley Ranch creates an urban experience similar to that of the Farmers' Market in Los Angeles.

several neighborhoods and the Green Valley Athletic Club signified that Green Valley had arrived. Contributing to the community's popularity was the Greenspun family's and Fine's penchant for trying new and unique things, like promoting events within the residential area to build a sense of community and commissioning J. Seward Johnson to build lifelike sculptures on several street corners. The great success of the community is best exemplified by a touching story told by Hank Greenspun's son Brian: In the late 1980s, when Hank Greenspun was dying, Brian drove him out to look at Green Valley. He doubted that his father had ever imagined this place—Greenspun said he actually had, but that he expected it to come to fruition only in his great-grandchildren's time.

Since his death, Greenspun's Green Valley has expanded to include Green Valley Ranch, which currently comprises four residential develop-

ments. The new community is home to the most elaborate of the Station Casinos and to the 400,000-square-foot, $80 million District at Green Valley Ranch. On the ground floor of the District are dozens of fine retail stores, as well as a variety of dining and street entertainers, and above are two stories of lofts, flats, and office space for sale. The president of the development company, John Kilduff, described the District very succinctly: "It's not a mall. It's Main Street USA."

Thanks to the residential revolution started by Green Valley in this area, Henderson is now one of the fastest-growing cities in the United States—second only to Las Vegas itself. Henderson now tops a population of a quarter of a million, and Green Valley now boasts 8,400 acres and 75,000 residents—holding strong its reputation as the master of master-planned communities in southern Nevada.

Castillo del Sol (Dr. Lonnie Hammargren's House)

Dr. Lonnie Hammargren is a Las Vegas neurosurgeon with a long history of community involvement, but even after a term as lieutenant governor, he is still better known for his house. Hammargren bought his house in a fashionable suburban neighborhood in 1969. Since then, the neighborhood has changed very little, but Hammargren's house has changed a lot.

In order to better pursue his interest in astronomy, for example, Hammargren added an observatory and planetarium. Now the observatory boasts not just one of Nevada's largest telescopes, but also a large collection of boxing memorabilia, and the planetarium includes a large dinosaur model and Native American artifacts. The good doctor's world of wonders also includes such random items as: a piano that belonged to Liberace, art by noted Western artist Roy Purcell, a scarf that belonged to Mama Cass Elliot, a bag that was owned by Janis Joplin, artifacts from New Guinea, a swimming pool with a mural of the Challenger Space Shuttle astronauts, motorcycles and bicycles that belonged to Hollywood stars, and a plethora of articles from Nevada, the Southwest, Venice, Mesoamerica, Russia, and Asia.

Hammargren now calls his home Castillo Del Sol, "Castle of the Sun," because the entrance area is modeled after the Castillo pyramid on Mexico's Yucatan Peninsula. He occasionally holds an open house, but it takes a few visits to get through all of it. As any Las Vegan will testify, though, an afternoon at the doctor's is a little wacky, but well worth the time.

Temple Beth Sholom

A few Jews lived in Las Vegas during its early years, but not until 1946 did the city's first congregation, that of Temple Beth Sholom, make its presence felt with its own temple downtown. Since then, the city's Jewish community has grown considerably. Current estimates of the Clark County Jewish population range as high as 100,000, with at least 18 synagogues.

From the beginning, Temple Beth Sholom's community was unique, a meeting place for the old (presumably more respectable) and new (gaming-oriented) Las Vegas. For example, Moe Dalitz of the Desert Inn and Jack Entratter of the Sands were active members, as were several other casino operators. But joining them were attorneys like David Zenoff and businessmen like Lloyd Katz, who operated movie theaters and, with his wife Edythe, played a key role in the Jewish Federation and other organizations.

As Las Vegas changed, so did its Jewish community. The addition of newer temples around town, an aging building at Beth Sholom, and a general exodus of its members out to Summerlin eventually led Temple Beth Sholom to consider moving, too. The congregation bought seven acres of land in Summerlin, and the new Temple Beth Sholom was dedicated there on September 24, 2000. The $10 million complex includes a sanctuary with seating for more than 1,600 worshipers, social halls, a religious school, a mosaic made of Jerusalem stone, and a Warsaw Ghetto Remembrance Garden. Even as Las Vegas' Jewish communities continue to expand, Temple Beth Sholom remains the oldest and most prominent, now counting over 600 member families.

The Jerusalem stone used to build the outer facade of the temple walls was brought straight from Israel.

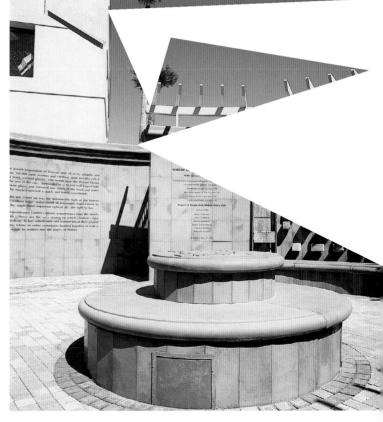

Warsaw Ghetto Remembrance Garden, built with hundreds of stones imported directlly from the Warsaw Ghetto.

Las Vegas High School

Today, Las Vegas High School is on East Sahara, and its old building at 7th and Bridger houses the local performing arts high school. For many years, though, the old building was Las Vegas' only high school. Its history begins in 1927, when Las Vegas officials hired a new school superintendent, Maude Frazier, who immediately pointed up the need for a new, larger high school. She proposed to build a $350,000 facility that could accommodate 500 students. Las Vegans were shocked at the high cost, Frazier's notion that Las Vegas would actually have 500 high school students someday, and her plan to build it two blocks east of Fremont Street—which made it seem so far out of town. Frazier nevertheless managed to persuade the school board and the voters, and the school opened downtown in 1930.

Frazier's school would be the only high school in the area for nearly a quarter of a century, and it had a large impact on the town. It housed the first college-level classes offered in Las Vegas, and its athletic events became community events, especially when the 1944 football team went undefeated. Many Las Vegas High graduates went on to become prominent leaders, including Governor and US Senator Richard Bryan; Bob Faiss, who became one of the world's leading experts on gaming law; and Bill Morris, a lawyer and businessman who was so closely identified with his alma mater that he shared the nickname of the school's sports teams: Wildcat.

The building is notable for its Art Deco architecture, and is on the National Register of Historic Places. The neighborhood is a historic district, too, with many single-family residences built from the time of the Great Depression to the end of World War II, especially in the Tudor Revival, Mission, and Ranch styles. A significant number of the old houses have preserved their original appearances, even though they have been converted into professional offices.

Guardian Angel Cathedral

Sitting in the shadow of the Strip is the Guardian Angel Cathedral, opened as a shrine in 1963 and designated a cathedral 13 years later by Pope Paul VI. Its mosaics, 2,000-square-foot acrylic mural, and 12 stained glass windows are all the work of Hungarian artists Isabel and Edith Piczek, who also worked on the oldest church in Los Angeles and on the National Shrine of the Immaculate Conception in Washington, DC. One of Isabel Piczek's stained glass windows stands out in particular: it depicts the Las Vegas skyline in the 1970s, when she designed it.

The cathedral's unusual history and appearance are a good reflection of the strange history of the Catholic Diocese of Nevada. It was established in 1931, making Nevada the last of the 48 contiguous states to receive its own diocese. The diocese was not divided until 1995, when Las Vegas and Reno were separated. Today, the Catholic church in Las Vegas numbers an estimated 400,000 members, and its services are packed, thanks in part to the large influx of Latinos during the last quarter-century.

Guggenheim Hermitage Museum

The words Las Vegas don't make many people think of art. Yet Las Vegas has been the subject of study by architectural critics and historians. The *real* city has a thriving cultural community, including a symphony, an art museum, an art district, and plans for a downtown arts center, as well as an array of productions and exhibits both temporary and permanent at local museums, the University of Nevada, Las Vegas, and the Community College of Southern Nevada. Thanks to Steve Wynn and a partnership between Sheldon Adelson's Venetian and the Guggenheim Museum, art is also now a major Strip attraction.

Adelson originally teamed with the Guggenheim on two museums. One was the Guggenheim Las Vegas, which opened with "The Art of the Motorcycle," a brilliant collection of modern art that drew too few customers and too many groans, as if to say, "art in Las Vegas *would* focus on this kind of thing." Unfortunately, the Guggenheim Las Vegas eventually closed, but the other museum, the Guggenheim Hermitage, survived and thrived. The hermitage was a collaboration between the Solomon R. Guggenheim Foundation and the Russian Federation. It houses great works from the Guggenheim Collection in New York and the Hermitage Collection in Russia, and hosts temporary exhibitions from all over the world.

The Guggenheim Las Vegas unveiled in 2001 with "The Art of the Motorcycle Exhibition".

Las Vegas Bike Fest at Cashman Field Center.

Cashman Field Center

As Ed Von Tobel, Jr., the son of a pioneer Las Vegas businessman, noted, the Cashman Field Center came into being because "[i]t was hard to say no to Big Jim." In the 1930s, Big Jim Cashman, a local entrepreneur who was active in politics and the community, joined with other men from his Elks Lodge to start Helldorado, an annual Western celebration that included parades, a rodeo, and other entertainment. In order to give the event a permanent home, they built a stadium at Las Vegas Boulevard North and Washington, and named it Cashman Field.

In addition to hosting Helldorado events once a year, Cashman Field has been home to two baseball teams: the Las Vegas Wranglers in the 1940s and '50s, a minor league baseball team at the Class C level—a level so low that it has long since disappeared—and, more recently, the 51s, a AAA team more suitable to the city's current size. Special events such as the annual Big League Weekend, when major league teams play exhibition games just before the regular season, are also held at Cashman Field Center.

The nearly 10,000-seat stadium does more than just host baseball games. Indeed, local officials added "Center" to the field's name in recognition of the fact that it included more than just a stadium. The 55-acre complex offers 100,000 square feet of exhibit space for conventions ranging from bike rallies to retail companies, and its nearly 2,000-seat theater hosts community events, local theatrical productions, and touring Broadway shows.

Las Vegas Nevada (Mormon) Temple

Mormons were the first whites to settle in Las Vegas, but they left within three years of their arrival in 1855. The history of the Mormons from the 1920s, however, is an excellent example of the recent, stunningly rapid growth of southern Nevada: In the 1920s, Las Vegas finally counted enough Mormons to justify the creation of a ward. In 1954, the city's first Mormon stake (as a collection of several wards is called) was dedicated. Today, the Mormon church in Las Vegas includes 15 stakes, with another three in Henderson, one in North Las Vegas, and one in Logandale, and counts a total of 167 wards—almost all created in the last half century. Mormons now make up about seven percent of the population of the city—not much compared to the non-Mormon population, but much higher than the national average of about two percent.

Las Vegas' enormous growth qualified it for the next step beyond a stake: In 1984, the Church of Jesus Christ of Latter-Day Saints announced plans for its 43rd temple in the world, to be located in Las Vegas. Late the following year they broke ground in the shadow of Frenchman Mountain on the east side of Las Vegas. Four years and $18 million later, the Las Vegas Mormon community had its house of worship. Not only is it large, with more than 80,000 square feet of space and 192 rooms, but it's positively breathtaking with six spires, one of which is 119 feet high and topped with a 10-foot gold-leaf statue of the Angel Moroni.

Just as the Mormon Temple watches over Las Vegas, the Mormon church and its members have achieved considerable influence in southern Nevada. Senator Harry Reid, the Senate minority leader, is Mormon. His son Rory Reid and another Mormon, Bruce Woodbury, are two of the most influential members of the Clark County Commission. Richard Bunker, who comes from a Mormon family that has included a US senator, a city councilman, and several local business leaders, has himself been an influential leader in gaming regulation and the Colorado River Commission. Considering the Mormon church began in 1830 with only six members and faced violent oppression during most of its early years, the Las Vegas Mormon community's survival and growth—like that of Las Vegas itself—is proof of enormous perseverance and potential for even greater success.

Clark County Museum

The Clark County Museum has been a popular spot to learn about—and to touch—southern Nevada's history for more than 30 years. In the 1970s, a group of Henderson residents got together and drew up plans for a museum. From its tiny original building, a large complex has grown on the south end of Boulder Highway, now consisting of several buildings.

The main building houses the museum's exhibits, including a timeline of southern Nevada history, Native American artifacts, and old dresses once sold at a downtown Las Vegas clothing store. The museum's popular "hands-on" material includes everything from stones used for cooking by Native Americans to an old slot machine, and the rotating gallery has featured

General store from Last Frontier Village, a Western-themed amusement park/museum at the Frontier hotel-casino in the 1950s, now on display at the Ghost Town exhibit.

everything from classic photos of Las Vegas entertainers to the museum's collection of vintage mining stock certificates.

The other buildings that comprise the museum provide additional, unique ways to examine the past. The old Boulder City railroad depot, now located on the museum site, features a train out front and all sorts of other things one would expect to find at a train station inside, such as old equipment and baggage from the same time period as the depot. Another exhibit, called Heritage Street, offers visitors the opportunity to explore a collection of classic, preserved buildings, each from a different period in Nevada's history. One house is from the Tonopah-Goldfield mining boom of the early

Toll cabin from Lamoille, Nevada, at the Ghost Town exhibit.

*Jail from Tuscarora, Nevada, at
the Ghost Town exhibit*

twentieth century; another is from the Basic Townsite (now Henderson); and there's an old print shop named for Don Reynolds, longtime owner of the *Las Vegas Review-Journal*. Recent additions at the museum include the historic Grand Canyon Airlines ticket office building from Boulder City, and one of the cottages that the San Pedro, Los Angeles & Salt Lake Railroad built for its workers in 1911.

The Clark County Museum is also responsible for other historic county programs: North of the museum is the Clark County Wetlands Park, a throwback to the days when Las Vegas really was "the Meadows." The Searchlight Museum in the Searchlight Community Center traces the history of that town. The Howard W. Cannon Aviation Museum—named for a four-term US senator from Nevada who was also a World War II pilot and later a nationally recognized expert on defense issues—is above the baggage claim area at McCarran International Airport, and the museum tends other exhibits scattered around the airport as well. With all its offerings, projects, and programs, the Clark County Museum proves that the past remains very much a part of the present in Las Vegas.

Donald W. Reynolds Broadcast Center

At the West Charleston campus of the Community College of Southern Nevada, the Donald W. Reynolds Broadcast Center houses Las Vegas' two public radio stations, KNPR-89.5 FM and KCNV-89.7.

KNPR-89.5 FM signed onto the air on March 24, 1980, becoming the first National Public Radio (NPR) affiliate in Nevada. For many years, KNPR aired from a small building on the grounds of Sam's Town hotel-casino. As long as the hotel had no need for the space, the owner, Boyd Gaming, let the station use the property for free. But the desire for its own building, and Boyd's need to expand, eventually prompted a fund-raising drive and an application for financial support from the Donald W. Reynolds Foundation. That application was successful, and in 1998 the NPR station moved into its new building, named for Reynolds.

Over the years, the station has expanded into rural areas, so that it now serves a listenership in over 89,000 square miles of territory in Nevada, California, and Arizona. In 2003, KNPR moved to 88.9 on the dial and went to a 24-hour news and talk format. At the same time, Las Vegas saw a major expansion with the creation of its second radio station, KCNV-89.7, which plays almost entirely classical music.

Las Vegas Art Museum

Bret Price's XO, 2000, *adorns the west side of the Las Vegas Art Museum building.*

As Steve Wynn's collection at the Wynn Las Vegas, the Guggenheim museum in the Venetian, and the many other galleries along the Strip attest, fine art has become part of the tourist experience in Las Vegas. But art is also part of the real city that surrounds the Strip. Miles west of the neon lights, near the Lakes and Peccole Ranch residential developments, the Las Vegas Art Museum is proof that there really is a cultured side to Sin City.

The Las Vegas Art Museum was born in 1950 as the Las Vegas Art League. For many years, the museum was housed in a building in Lorenzi Park, near the Nevada State Museum and Historical Society. In the 1980s and '90s, the longtime director of the Las Vegas-Clark County Library District, Charles Hunsberger, embarked on a controversial building program that would turn the city's libraries into much more than book-lending facilities. The buildings were renovated to make them more esthetic, and internet connections and other new, modern modes of learning were introduced. As part of the libraries' new image as full community centers, the Las Vegas Art Museum was invited to move into the Sahara West Library in 1997. That "merger" created the Sahara West Library/Las Vegas Art Museum of which Las Vegans are so fond today. In 2002, the museum became a Smithsonian affiliate, and it now hosts a variety of exhibitions, lectures, and events.

Beyond the Lights: Day-Trips from Las Vegas

Lost City Museum of Archaeology

The Lost City Museum in Overton draws attention to some of the earliest residents of southern Nevada, the Anasazi. In some Native American languages, the name Anasazi means "ancestral people"; in other Native American languages it refers to ancient enemies. The Anasazi made their homes primarily in New Mexico, Arizona, Colorado, and Utah, but they spilled over just a bit across the Colorado River into Nevada.

The Anasazi built large pueblos to live in, and sustained themselves from farming, setting up their own irrigation systems with ditches and canals. They also traded with other native tribes, made baskets, and mined salt and turqoise. Interestingly, archaeologists have found that the tribe even had a form of gambling, a game that might resemble keno or bingo—hardly a surprise in these parts.

The Anasazi dwelled in southern Nevada for about 800 years before disappearing from their homes around 1150—about the time the Toltec Empire in central Mexico collapsed, sending waves of economic and political change

Previous page: Sunrise over the Grand Canyon, as seen from Yaki Point off of Desert View Drive.

throughout the Southwest. Some theorize that the Nevadan Anasazi merged or fought with the Paiutes, but no evidence exists to support either assertion. The Anasazi are ancestors of the Hopi, so they may simply have joined with that Arizona tribe.

The place where they lived near the Colorado seems to have been a substantial city. Anthropologist Mark Harrington, then of the Museum of the American Indian in New York City and later curator of the Southwest Museum of Los Angeles, led the first excavation in 1924 with Governor James Scrugham of Nevada, who apparently called the site "Pueblo Grande de Nevada." In 1933, the National Park Service asked Harrington to return to supervise a final excavation. With Hoover Dam under construction, the waters of Lake Mead were rising and Pueblo Grande would soon disappear, presumably forever. Harrington and workers from the Civilian Conservation Corps (CCC) worked all the way up until the water started rising around them.

The park service and CCC then built the Lost City Museum to house the artifacts they found there. In 1953, the museum was turned over to the state, which now maintains it as a park and museum for research, exhibits, and tours that take visitors back into the past . . . *way* back.

Large pueblos built by the Anasazi tribe as dwellings.

Jean

Two hotels belonging to Mandalay Resort Group greet visitors to Jean, about 22 miles south of Las Vegas. But while the hotels are the most visible and welcome part of the hamlet along Interstate 15, the town's history is actually rich and interesting as well.

Jean's significance has always been that it is on the road to Los Angeles. It is the site at which construction was completed on the San Pedro, Los Angeles & Salt Lake Railroad in 1905. To celebrate the achievement, Mrs. R. E. Wells, wife of the railroad's general manager, had a gold spike made, and on January 30 chief engineer Edward Tilton pushed it into the tracks with his thumb to signify the railroad's official completion. Within a few years, the town had a railroad station and a post office, and thus served as a stop-off for travelers to and from nearby mining areas like Goodsprings, and as a supply point for that camp's miners.

Later on, Jean became known for Pop's Oasis, a small bar and casino owned by Peter Simon. Pop's was a popular place for travelers to take a break, and it earned a reputation for its display of the car in which Bonnie and Clyde were riding when they were shot. Simon and his partners eventually built two hotel-casinos, the Gold Strike and Nevada Landing, which Circus Circus Enterprises bought for $725 million in 1995. A decade later, both establishments welcome travelers and tour buses into their smaller, less hectic atmospheres, located just up the highway from the hustle and bustle of the Strip.

Laughlin

Don Laughlin got his start in the gambling business while still in high school, where he ran a punchboard game. He had already owned and sold three Las Vegas casinos when, in 1966, he happened upon a bar with a few motel rooms attached while wandering along an unpaved road along the Colorado River. He noted that the location had a built-in market: travelers along nearby roads, residents of Bullhead City across the Arizona line, and visitors to the Lake Mead National Recreation Area. Even so, the current bar owners had gone bankrupt, so Laughlin bought the property.

Since he was the only business owner in the vicinity, the community that grew up around him became known as Laughlin. That was only fair, because Laughlin really was responsible for the area's success: he expanded his Riverside Resort from eight motel rooms (only four of which were available to customers, since he and his family lived in the other four) to its current 1,400, plus spaces for 800 recreational vehicles—a market he emphasized when many others still doubted its profitability. He also started the town's first bank, bought the nearby airport, built and funded the bridge that crosses Davis Dam to replace the perilous road that once led into town. Today, the town of Laughlin has more than 10,000 hotel and motel rooms, Don Laughlin's casinos now have eight big-name neighbors, and the name Laughlin is beloved all around.

Primm

When travelers cross the border to Nevada from California, they are often looking for entertainment and gambling. Lucky for them, they don't have to go far at all: right across the border lies Primm. The town used to be known simply as Stateline, because it is right smack on the line between the states of California and Nevada. Since there's another Stateline in northern Nevada, though, things could get kind of confusing, so Primm was renamed for the entrepreneur who began it.

Before coming to Primm, Ernest Primm ran a casino called Primadonna in Reno, where he fought the city's effort to limit casinos to just one area. When he saw a chance to expand in the early 1950s, he went well beyond Reno's borders, paying about $15,000 for 400 acres of land in southern Nevada, then obtaining 400 more. On the California-Nevada line, his land included Whiskey Pete's Hotel and Casino, originally a 12-room motel and a tiny casino. Ernest's son Gary added two more resorts, the Primadonna and Buffalo Bill's, with entertainment, dining, shopping, two championship golf courses, a 100-foot-high Ferris wheel, and a roller coaster. By the mid-1990s, the Primms controlled about 2,600 hotel rooms and employed 3,500 workers in Nevada. Estimates place Primm's current population at about 500—all resort employees and their families.

Gary Primm expanded into Las Vegas when he teamed up with MGM to build the New York–New York hotel-casino. In 1999, Kirk Kerkorian bought out all of Primm's holdings, including those in his namesake town.

Mesquite

As with much of southern Nevada, Mesquite's history has a great deal to do with Mormons, the federal government, and tourism. Located in the Virgin River Valley, Mesquite was a stop along the Old Spanish Trail from New Mexico to California, and along the Mormon Road from Salt Lake to southern California. Settlements grew up around it, and in the 1880s and '90s Mormon settlers won an uphill battle to farm the land here. Mesquite residents soon opened motels and campgrounds for travelers, and built dairies for nearby farms.

In the early 1970s, the federal government completed Interstate 15, making travel through the area much easier. Beginning in the early 1980s, one entrepreneur after another recognized the desirability of the site along the highway. Accordingly, one motel, truck stop, restaurant, golf course, and RV park after another began popping up in Mesquite. Now, the town's estimated population is already more than 16,000, and it has become a favorite getaway for Las Vegans and a popular spot for out-of-town conventions.

Evidence of Searchlight's mining past.

Searchlight

Searchlight started out as a mining town, then became a pit stop in the desert. Prospectors had searched for gold in the desert west of the Colorado River for decades, but it was not until 1896 that serious efforts began to develop what would become Searchlight. The area's mining claims became the Quartette mine, and the Searchlight Mining District was formed in 1898. The strange name of the town has been much debated, but it seems most probable that it can be traced back to miner George Colton. According to one story, Colton lit a Searchlight match in the dark just to light his pipe so he could smoke—and suddenly he saw ore. In another account, tired of a fruitless search for ore, Colton said, "There is something here, boys, but it would take a searchlight to find it."

For about a decade and a half, Searchlight was a thriving mining town. It even challenged the new railroad town, Las Vegas, for the right to be county seat when Clark County was created in 1909. But the town was in decline by the 1920s, and even though its mines were revived a few times, it never approached the prosperity it enjoyed early in the twentieth century. Today, its population is still well under 1,000.

Drill Rock, once used for 4th of July drilling contests in which miners would compete to see who could double-jack or single-jack drill the fastest.

If Searchlight has a claim to fame, then it's probably one of the people who lived here: Legendary Hollywood costume designer Edith Head's stepfather was a mine superintendent here, and she spent time here as a girl. One of the Hollywood stars for whom Edith designed clothing was Clara Bow, the popular 1920s movie star whose charisma earned her the nickname "the It Girl." Bow married cowboy actor Rex Bell and they also moved to Searchlight, where they owned a ranch.

The most prominent Searchlight native is also its chronicler. Harry Reid, the son of a hard-rock miner, was born here and used to hitchhike his way to high school in Henderson. That determination to better himself sent Reid on to college and law school, then he rose in politics: assemblyman, lieutenant governor, Gaming Commission chairman (at the time federal and state officials were trying to force out the mob), congressman, and finally US senator. In 2004, his Democratic colleagues elected him Senate minority leader, making him one of the most powerful people in his party, if not the most powerful. In public speeches, Reid often refers to his upbringing in Searchlight. He knows a lot more about the town than just that, though: In 1998, the University of Nevada Press published his book, *Searchlight: The Camp that Didn't Fail.* Needless to say, the home Reid built for himself in Searchlight is a far cry from the rickety old shack he grew up in.

Sunset over the Grand Canyon, as seen from Hopi Point off of Hermit Road.

The Grand Canyon

Russell Baker, the Pulitzer Prize-winning columnist for *The New York Times,* once wrote a column called "Impressions of America" that was a series of one-liners about various places. For the Grand Canyon, Baker wrote: "Zeus and Moses each telling the other, 'And I thought I'd seen everything!'" Indeed, it is a sight to behold, and many visitors take a day trip out from Las Vegas to fly over the gaping gorge or to camp on-site.

Geologists estimate that the Grand Canyon is six to 12 million years old. At least, that is how long the Colorado, the nation's wildest river, has been cutting through it. The canyon is 277 miles long, as much as 18 miles wide, and at least 5,000 feet deep—that is, almost a mile. One group of Native Americans, the Havasupai, has dwelled in the canyon for more than 800 years. The first Europeans to view it apparently belonged to a party led by García López de Cárdenas, who was scouting on behalf of a Spanish explorer, Francisco Coronado. Father Francisco Garcés, a Spanish missionary who traveled through the Southwest in the 1770s, noticed that dirt had made the water look red, and so he named the river *Colorado*, "ruddy" or "red."

Theodore Roosevelt was the first president to push through legislation protecting parts of the Grand Canyon from encroachment. The canyon is one of the seven natural wonders of the world, and the area became a national park in 1919, to which more land was added several times during the twentieth century. The site is and has always been a major attraction for tourists, and future visitors should heed the advice of veteran canyon-visitors and remember to be careful: that first step down is a big one.

Sunrise over the Grand Canyon, as seen from Yaki Point off of Desert View Drive.

Mojave Desert

All those who doubt that a desert can be beautiful need to get themselves to the Mojave.

It covers more than 25,000 square miles of southeastern California and southern Nevada, plus a little bit of southwestern Utah and northwestern Arizona. To the north lies the Great Basin, beginning with the Sierra Nevada mountain range and extending to the Wasatch Mountains near Salt Lake City; to the southwest are the San Gabriel-San Bernardino mountains; and the Colorado River Plateau is to the east.

While the Mojave Desert is the site of the famed Death Valley—named for the terror it struck into an emigrant party in the late 1840s—the desert actually contains a lot of life. About 200 plant species, including a variety of cacti, yucca, and sagebrush, survive there with only about five inches of rainfall each year. During the summer monsoon season, flash floods through desert washes are typical, which is why many Las Vegans joke (not entirely kidding) that they do indeed get five inches of rain each year, but it usually all comes in one day. The lack of both food and water in the region has made survival difficult throughout the centuries for the Southern Paiutes, the major Native American tribe of the Mojave Desert.

Two national parks lie within the Mojave Desert: One is Death Valley National Park, whose 3.3 million acres include the continent's lowest, most arid land. 550 square miles of the park are below sea level, and the lowest point in the Western Hemisphere, at 282 feet below sea level, can be found near the Badwater area. The Furnace Creek Inn and Ranch is a favorite place for park visitors to stay. A favorite attraction at the park is Scotty's Castle, even though the two-story Spanish-style villa isn't really a castle. In fact, neither did the home ever belong to Walter Scott, the self-promoter known as "Death Valley Scotty," but it was owned by a friend of his. The other national park in Nevada's Mojave, called Joshua Tree, is shared with southern California. The park is named for the unusual plant most often seen in the Mojave Desert, which supposedly was named by Mormon pioneers who imagined the tree's uplifted branches to be waving them on toward their Promised Land, like the Old Testament prophet Joshua.

Abandoned house, Cima, Mojave National Reserve, California.

Index